Macmillan McGraw-Hill

TEXAS Mathematics

k

Volume 1

Authors

Altieri • Balka • Day • Gonsalves • Grace • Krulik
Malloy • Molix-Bailey • Moseley • Mowry • Myren
Price • Reynosa • Santa Cruz • Silbey • Vielhaber

Macmillan
McGraw-Hill

About the Cover

Texas Focus The "Texas Hill Country" is a scenic 14,000 square mile area located in the heart of Texas that includes all or part of twenty-five counties. This region contains small towns, natural springs, rolling hills, caves, and pastures. Abundant wildlife such as white-tailed deer, mockingbirds, horses, and armadillos make their home among the hills. In the spring, open fields are dotted with colorful wildflowers such as the Texas state flower, the Bluebonnet.

Mathematics Focus Two of the main topics in Kindergarten are patterns and position. There are many patterns in the picnic scene on the cover. Ask students to describe the patterns they see. Have students use words such as near/far to describe the position of the butterfly or stream, above/below to describe the apples on the tree or the picnic basket, right/left to describe the tree and horses.

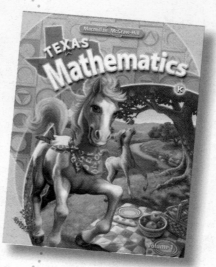

Macmillan McGraw-Hill

The *McGraw-Hill* Companies

Send all inquiries to:
Macmillan/McGraw-Hill
8787 Orion Place
Columbus, OH 43240-4027

Volume 1
ISBN: 978-0-02-105746-7
MHID: 0-02-105746-X

Printed in the United States of America.

6 7 8 9 10 RMN/LEH 16 15 14 13 12 11

Contents in Brief

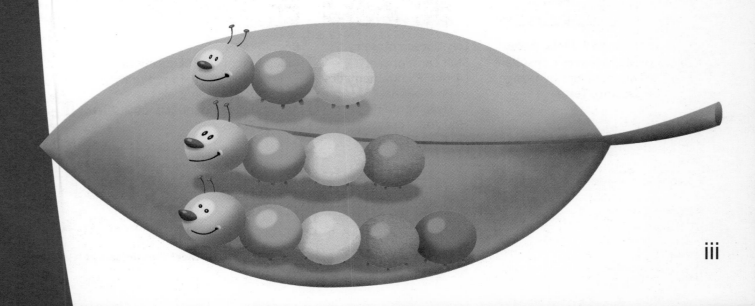

Mary Behr Altieri
Putnam/Northern
    Westchester BOCES
Yorktown Heights,
    New York

Don S. Balka
Professor Emeritus
Saint Mary's College
Notre Dame, Indiana

Roger Day, Ph.D.
Mathematics Department Chair
Pontiac Township High School
Pontiac, Illinois

Philip D. Gonsalves
Mathematics Coordinator
Alameda County Office
    of Education and
    California State
    University East Bay
Hayward, California

Ellen C. Grace
Consultant
Albuquerque,
    New Mexico

Stephen Krulik
Mathematics Consultant
Cherry Hill, New Jersey

Carol E. Malloy
Assistant Professor of
    Mathematics Education
University of North
    Carolina at Chapel Hill
Chapel Hill, North
    Carolina

Rhonda J. Molix-Bailey
Mathematics Consultant
Mathematics by Design
Desoto, Texas

Lois Gordon Moseley
Staff Developer
NUMBERS: Mathematics
    Professional
    Development
Houston, Texas

Brian Mowry
Independent Math Educational
    Consultant/Part-Time Pre-K
    Instructional Specialist
Austin Independent School District
Austin, Texas

Christina L. Myren
Consultant Teacher
Conejo Valley Unified
    School District
Thousand Oaks, California

Jack Price
Professor Emeritus
California State
    Polytechnic University
Pomona, California

Mary Esther Reynosa
Instructional Specialist for
    Elementary Mathematics
Northside Independent
    School District
San Antonio, Texas

Rafaela M. Santa Cruz
SDSU/CGU Doctoral
    Program in Education
San Diego State University
San Diego, California

Robyn Silbey
Math Content Coach
Montgomery County
    Public Schools
Gaithersburg, Maryland

Kathleen Vielhaber
Mathematics Consultant
St. Louis, Missouri

Consulting and Contributing Authors

Margaret Kilgo
Consulting Author and
    Educational Consultant
Kilgo Consulting, Inc.
Austin, Texas

Donna J. Long
Mathematics Consultant
Indianapolis, Indiana

FOLDABLES **Dinah Zike**
Educational Consultant
Dinah-Might Activities, Inc.
San Antonio, Texas

Macmillan/McGraw-Hill wishes to thank the following professionals for their invaluable feedback during the development of the program. They reviewed a variety of instructional materials at different stages of development.

Julie Acosta
Math Coordinator
McAllen ISD
McAllen, Texas

Tita Alarcon
Elementary Curriculum
    Specialist
Plano ISD
Plano, Texas

Monica Arriaga
Instructional Specialist
Ryan Elementary
Laredo ISD
Laredo, Texas

Susie Bellah
Kindergarten Teacher
Lakeland Elementary
Humble ISD
Humble, Texas

Elizabeth Firmin Birdwell
Director of Curriculum and
    Instruction, PK–12
Duncanville ISD
Duncanville, Texas

Brooke Borer
Elementary Math Specialist
Northside ISD
San Antonio, Texas

Wendy Buchanan
3rd Grade Teacher
The Classical Center at Vial
Garland ISD
Garland, Texas

Ida Burkhart
5th Grade Teacher
R. L. Martin Elementary
Brownsville ISD
Brownsville, Texas

Carol S. Carter
PK-8 Math/Science
    Coordinator
Corsicana ISD
Corsicana, Texas

Patricia Delgado
Mathematics Strategist
Mercedes ISD
Mercedes, Texas

Sheila Q. Delony
3rd Grade Teacher
Maedgen Elementary
Lubbock ISD
Lubbock, Texas

Lorrie Drennon
Teacher/Curriculum
  Coordinator
Mildred ISD
Mildred, Texas

Carolyn Elender
District Math Instructional
  Specialist
Pasadena ISD
Pasadena, Texas

Anna Dahinden Flynn
5th Grade Teacher
Coulson Tough K-6 Flex
  School
Conroe ISD
The Woodlands, Texas

Irene C. Garcia
District Elementary Math
  Specialist
Midland ISD
Midland, Texas

Lucy Gijon
3rd Grade Bilingual Teacher
Vista Hills Elementary
Ysleta ISD
El Paso, Texas

Gail Brown Guthrie
Teacher
Huppertz Elementary School
San Antonio ISD
San Antonio, Texas

Ellen Hatley
Instructional Teacher for
  Elementary Mathematics
Northside ISD
San Antonio, Texas

Jennifer Houghton
Math Instruction Specialist
Palm Elementary
Austin ISD
Austin, Texas

Ty G. Jones
Accelerated Mathematics
    Instruction Specialist
Lancaster ISD
Lancaster, Texas

Frieda Lamprecht
Elementary Curriculum
    Specialist
Austin ISD
Austin, Texas

Leigh Ann Mewhirter
1st Grade Teacher
University Park Elementary
Highland Park ISD
Dallas, Texas

Susan Murphy
Assistant Principal
Christie Elementary
Frisco ISD
Frisco, Texas

Virginia A. Nwuba
Math Specialist
Tinsley Elementary School
Houston ISD
Houston, Texas

Cindy Pearson
5th Grade Teacher
John D. Spicer Elementary
Birdville ISD
Haltom City, Texas

Julia C. Perez
Elementary Math Content
    Specialist
Houston ISD
South Region
Houston, Texas

Lacy Prince
3rd Grade Vanguard Teacher
Pleasantville Elementary
Houston ISD
Houston, Texas

Dr. Karen Rhynard
Math Coordinator
Round Rock ISD
Round Rock, Texas

Jesusita I. Rios
District Bilingual Elementary
   Specialist
Edgewood ISD
San Antonio, Texas

Caroline Soderstrom
Elementary Teacher
O'Shea Keleher Elementary
Socorro ISD
El Paso, Texas

Dr. Jose Solis
Mathematics Dean K–12
Laredo ISD
Laredo, Texas

Alice B. Watkins
Math Specialist
DeZavala Elementary
Midland ISD
Midland, Texas

Maria L. Zsohar
Math Specialist
Richardson ISD
Richardson, Texas

Judy Rogers
Math Specialist,
   Instructional Division
Lubbock ISD
Lubbock, Texas

Consultants and Reviewers

Macmillan/McGraw-Hill wishes to thank the following professionals for their feedback. They were instrumental in providing valuable input toward the development of this program in these specific areas.

Mathematical Content

Gerald Kulm
Curtis D. Robert Professor
Texas A & M University
College Station, Texas

Leo Armando Ramirez, Sr.
Consultant/Author
Retired (McAllen High School)
McAllen, Texas

Assessment

Jane D. Gawronski
Director of Assessment and Outreach
San Diego State University
San Diego, California

Cognitive Guided Instruction

Susan B. Empson
Associate Professor of Mathematics
   and Science Education
University of Texas at Austin
Austin, Texas

English Learners

Cheryl Avalos
Mathematics Consultant
Los Angeles County Office of Education, Retired
Hacienda Heights, California

Kathryn Heinze
Graduate School of Education
Hamline University
St. Paul, Minnesota

Family Involvement

Paul Giganti, Jr.
Mathematics Education Consultant
Albany, California

Literature

David M. Schwartz
Children's Author, Speaker, Storyteller
Oakland, California

Problem Solving

Lydia Aranda
First Grade Teacher
Herff Elementary School
San Antonio, Texas

Susie Bellah
Kindergarten Teacher
Lakeland Elementary
Humble, Texas

Elizabeth Firmin Birdwell
Director of Curriculum and Instruction
Duncanville ISD
Duncanville, Texas

Brooke Borer
Elementary Math Specialist
Northside ISD
San Antonio, Texas

Anna Dahinden Flynn
5th Grade Math Teacher
Coulson Tough School
The Woodlands, Texas

Ellen D. Hatley
Instructional Teacher for Elementary Mathematics
Northside ISD
San Antonio, Texas

June Ann Hurt
First Grade Teacher
Gifted and Talented
Lamkin Elementary
Cypress, Texas

Jacqueline E. Navarro
Grade Level Chair, 1st Grade
Miguel Carrillo Elementary
San Antonio, Texas

Virginia A. Nwuba
Math Specialist
Tinsley Elementary School
HISD
Houston, Texas

Vertical Alignment

Berchie Holliday
National Educational Consultant
Silver Spring, Maryland

Deborah A. Hutchens, Ed.D.
Principal
Norfolk Highlands Elementary
Chesapeake, Virginia

Texas Reviewers

Each Texas reviewer reviewed at least two chapters of the Student Edition, giving feedback and suggestions for improving the effectiveness of the mathematics instruction.

Adelina Bazan-Alaniz
Coordinator for Mathematics
Mission C.I.S.D
Mission, TX

Sangeeta Bhattacharya
ESL Lead Teacher
Klentzman Intermediate School
Houston, TX

Lisa Bolte
Math Specialist
Southwest ISD
San Antonio, TX

Adriana Cantu
4th Grade Teacher
O'Shea Keleher Elementary
El Paso, TX

Carol S. Carter
PK–8 Math/Science Coordinator
Corsicana ISD
Corsicana, TX

William J. Comley
First Grade Teacher
Western Hills Primary
Fort Worth, TX

Mercy Cosper
First Grade Teacher
Pershing Park Elementary
Killeen, TX

Sheila Q. Delony
3rd Grade Teacher
Maedgen Elementary
Lubbock ISD
Lubbock, TX

Irene C. Garcia
District Elementary Math
 Specialist
Midland ISD
Midland, TX

Sylvia Hill, Ph.D.
Math Teacher
The Rice School
La Escuela Rice
Houston, TX

Juanita Hutto
Math Skills Specialist
Sammons Elementary
Houston, TX

Ty G. Jones
Accelerated Mathematics Instruction
 Specialist
Lancaster ISD
Lancaster, TX

Tekeisha Lee
Special Education Teacher
Classical Center at Vial Elementary
Garland, TX

Elizabeth T. Martinez
Bilingual Teacher
Lantrip Elementary
Houston, TX

Rashad Javed Rana
Math Coordinator
Donna ISD
Donna, TX

Judy Rogers
Math Specialist, Instructional
 Division
Lubbock ISD
Lubbock, TX

Delinda Martinez Sanchelli
ESL Lead Teacher
Klentzman Intermediate
Houston, TX

Velma Sanchez
Teacher
Franklin Elementary
PSJA ISD
Alamo, TX

Barbara J. Savage
1st Grade Teacher
University Park Elementary
Dallas, TX

Stacey L. Shapiro
Teacher
Zilker Elementary
Austin, TX

Mary J. Wick
Second Grade Teacher
Hanby Elementary School
Mesquite, TX

Maria L. Zsohar
Math Specialist
Richardson ISD
Richardson, TX

Contents

Start Smart

Compare and Sort Objects

Contents

CHAPTER 2 Use Numbers 0 to 5

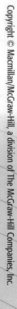

CHAPTER 3
Describe Position and Patterns

xv

Contents

Use Numbers to 10

CHAPTER 5 Construct and Use Graphs

Contents

CHAPTER 7 Compare Measurements

Contents

CHAPTER 8 Count by Ones to 100

CHAPTER 9 Use Time

Contents

CHAPTER 11 Model Addition

Contents

End-of-Year Projects

Student Handbook

WorkMat 1: Story Mat

WorkMat 2: Two-Part Mat

WorkMat 3: Graphing Mat

WorkMat 4: Sorting Mat

WorkMat 5: Ten-Frame

WorkMat 6: Ten-Frames

WorkMat 7: Part-Part-Whole

WorkMat 8: Number Lines

Texas

Start Smart

Let's Review!

Texas Mockingbird

Start Smart

Name: _____

Underlying Processes and Mathematical Tools

Let's dance!

Did you Know?
The square dance is the state dance of Texas.

Directions: Circle the vest that is beside the blue vest. X the skirt that is above the green boots. Underline the boots that are under the pink skirt.

Name: _____

Did you Know?

The Monarch butterfly is Texas' state butterfly.

Directions: Draw a line to match each butterfly to a flower.
Count each butterfly. Count each flower.

Bug Buddies

Directions: Draw a line to match the number of insects in a group with the same number of flowers.

Name: _____

START SMART 3

Patterns, Relationships, and Algebraic Thinking

Making Chili

Did you Know?

The state dish of Texas is chili.

Directions: Which food comes next in the pattern? Copy the pattern and draw the food that comes next.

What comes next?

1.

2.

3.

4.

Directions:
1–2. Circle the object that could come next in the pattern.
3–4. Draw the object that could come next in the pattern.

Name: _____

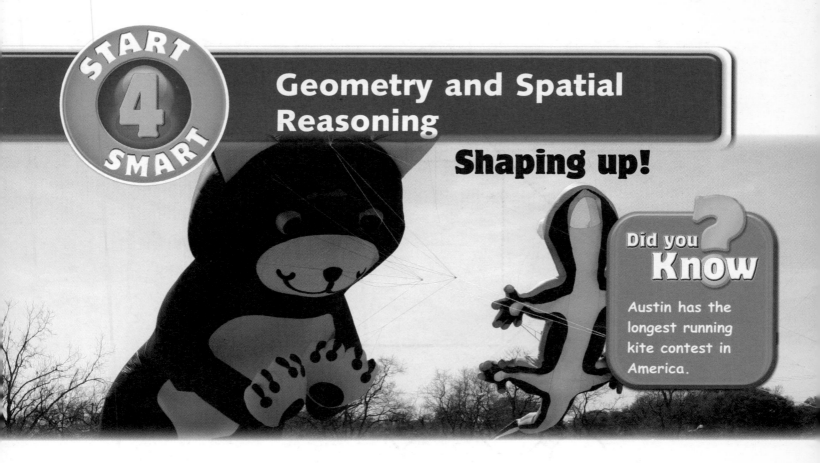

Geometry and Spatial Reasoning

Shaping up!

Did you Know?
Austin has the longest running kite contest in America.

Directions: Trace each shape. Finish coloring the shape.
Color each kite the same color as the shape it matches.

Let's go fly a kite! ·······································

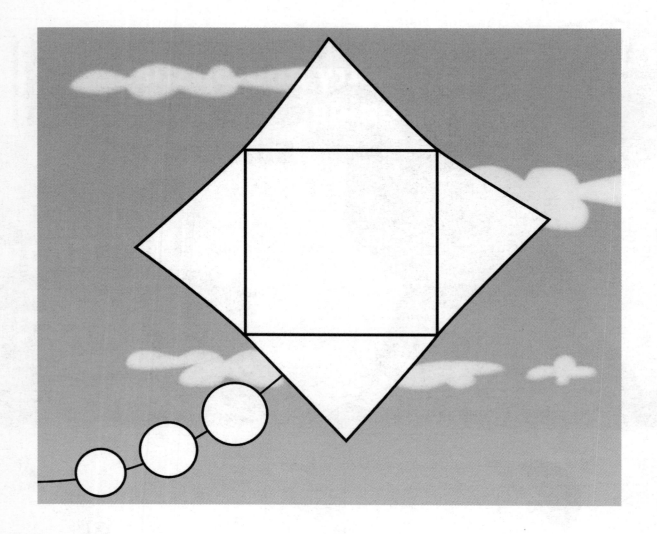

Directions: Color each circle green. Color each square blue. Color each triangle purple.
Draw a kite using a triangle, square, and circle.

Name: _____

Measurement

Hot, hot, hot!

Did you Know?

Smaller peppers are usually hotter than larger peppers.

Directions: Circle the pepper that is the smallest pepper on each plate.
Put an X on the pepper that is the largest pepper on each plate.

Which is longer?

Directions: Circle the object in each group that is longer.

Name: _____

Probability and Statistics

How many mockingbirds?

Did you Know?

The mockingbird is the state bird of Texas.

Directions: Use color tiles to show how many of each bird are in the tree.
Color a square on the graph to show how many of each.

At the Store

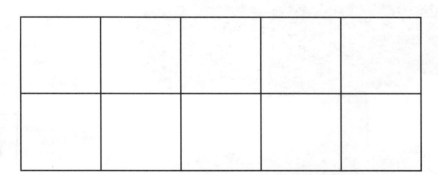

Directions: Color a square beside each object to show how many of that object there are in the store. Circle the photo that has more.

Compare and Sort Objects

Key Vocabulary

alike

different

sort

Explore

Circle the yellow flower.

✓ Are You Ready for Chapter 1?

1

2 🍎

3

4

Directions:
1. Trace the lines.
2. Circle the car. Put an X on the tree.
3. Color the truck red. Color the ball blue.
   Color the bird yellow. Color the flower purple.
4. Circle the object that is small.

This page checks skills needed for Chapter 1.

MATH at HOME

Dear Family,

Today my class started Chapter 1, **Compare and Sort Objects**.
I will be learning to sort objects and to match groups of objects.
Here are my vocabulary words, an activity to do, and a list of
books we can read together.

Love,
_____

Activity

Have your child help you sort laundry items, such as socks or food items such as canned goods.

Key Vocabulary

sort to group together items that have something in common

same number

Math Online   Click on the eGlossary link at tx.grKmath.com
to find out more about these words. There are 13 languages.

Books to Read

Dinosaurs Are Different
by Aliki
Harper Collins Children's Books,
1986.

Mixed-Up Chameleon
by Eric Carle
Harper Collins
Children's Books, 1984.

Is Your Mama a Llama?
by Deborah Guarino
Scholastic Press, 1997.

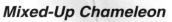

Estimada familia,

Hoy mi clase comenzó el Capítulo 1, **Compara y ordena objetos**. Aprenderé a ordenar objetos y a emparejar grupos de objetos. A continuación están mis palabras de vocabulario, una actividad que podemos realizar y una lista de libros que podemos leer juntos.

Cariños, _____

Actividad

Pídanle a su hijo(a) que les ayude a ordenar la ropa para lavar, como las medias; o los comestibles, como los alimentos enlatados.

Vocabulario clave

ordenar agrupar objectos que tienen algo en común.

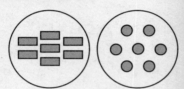

mismo número

Math Online Visiten el enlace eGlossary en tx.grKmath.com para averiguar más sobre estas palabras, las cuales se muestran en 13 idiomas.

Libros para leer

Los dinosaurios son diferentes
de Aliki
Editorial Juventud, 1996.

El camaleon camaleonico
de Eric Carle
Kokinos, 2005.

¿Tu mama es una llama?
de Deborah Guarino
Scholastic Trade, 1991.

Name _____

Alike and Different

Vocabulary

alike

different

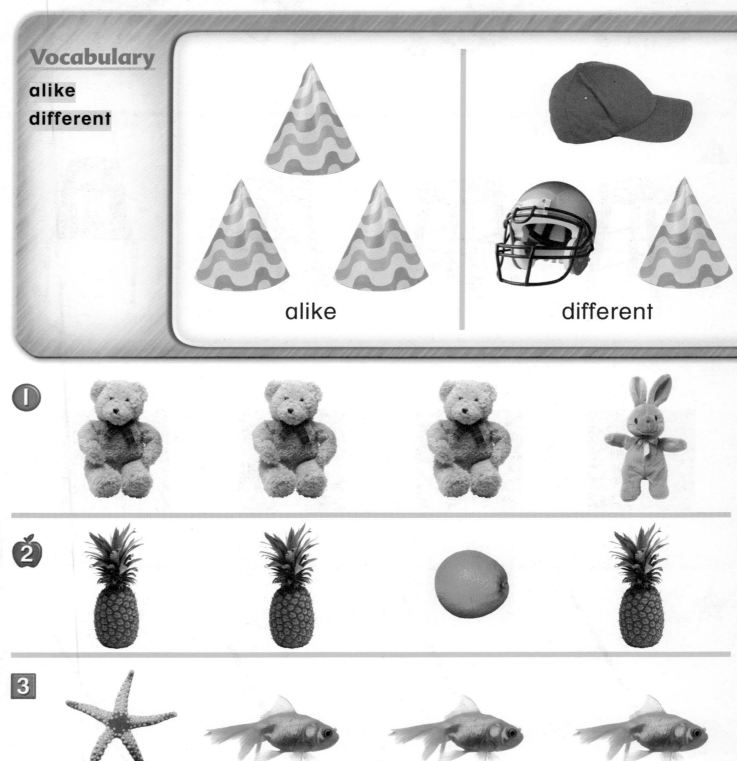

alike

different

1

2

3

Directions:

1–3. Compare the objects in each row. Circle the objects that are alike. Mark an X on the one that is different. Tell how you know.

4

5

6

 7

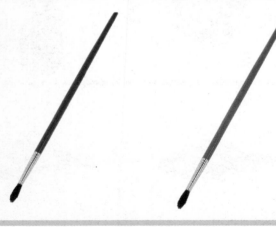  

Directions:
4–7. Compare the objects in each row. Circle the objects that are alike. Mark an X on the one that is different. Tell how you know.

Math at Home Activity: Draw a picture of some items in each room of your house. Ask your child to show which items are alike and different.

18   eighteen

Chapter 1   Lesson 1

Sort by One Attribute

Vocabulary

sort

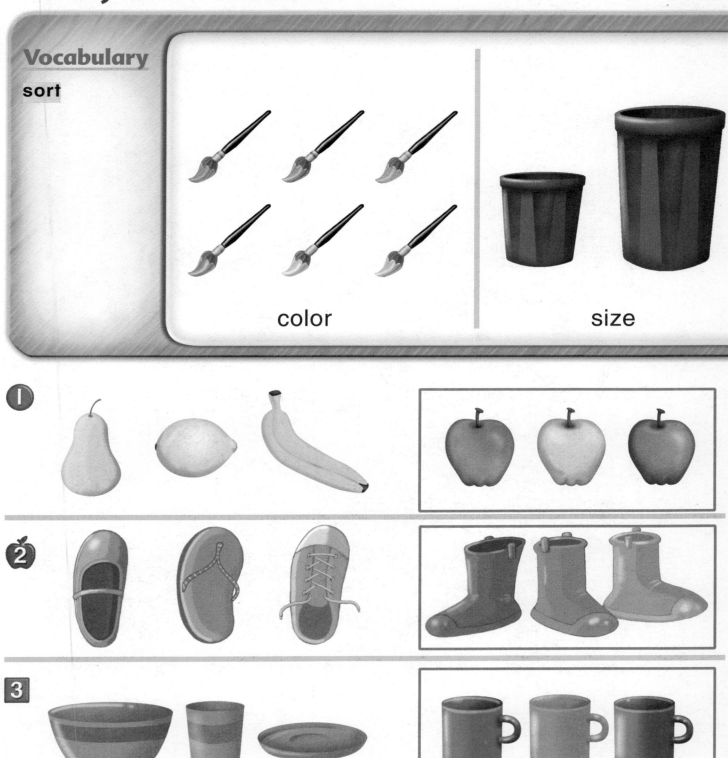

color   size

①

②

③

Directions:

1–3. Describe and identify each object in the row. Circle the object in the box that belongs in that row. Mark an X on the objects that do not belong. Tell how you know.

Directions: Sort the picnic items by size. Draw a line from each picnic item to the correct basket.

Math at Home Activity: Help your child sort toys by placing all the same color toys together. Then sort another way.

Name _____

Problem-Solving Strategy
Act It Out

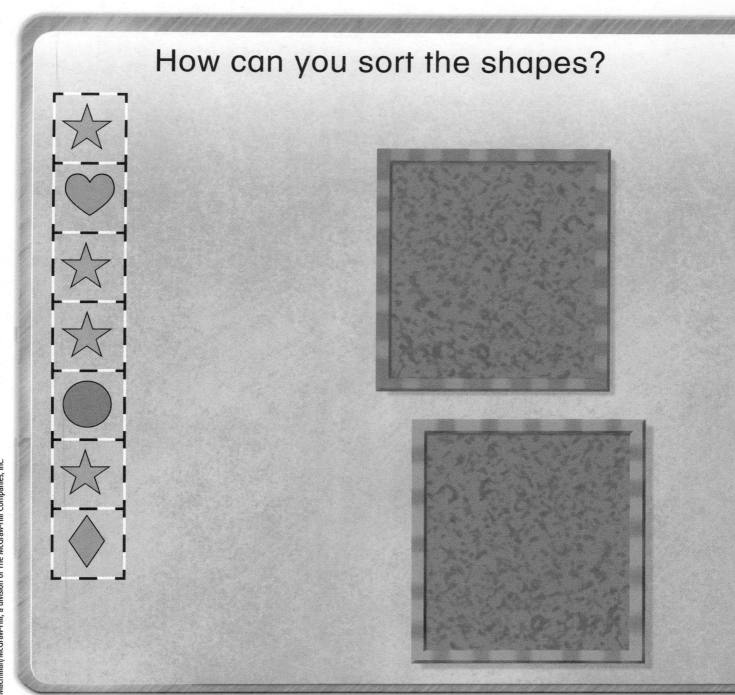

How can you sort the shapes?

Directions: Cut out the shapes. Glue shapes that are alike on one bulletin board. Glue shapes that are different on the other bulletin board. Explain to a classmate how you sorted the objects.

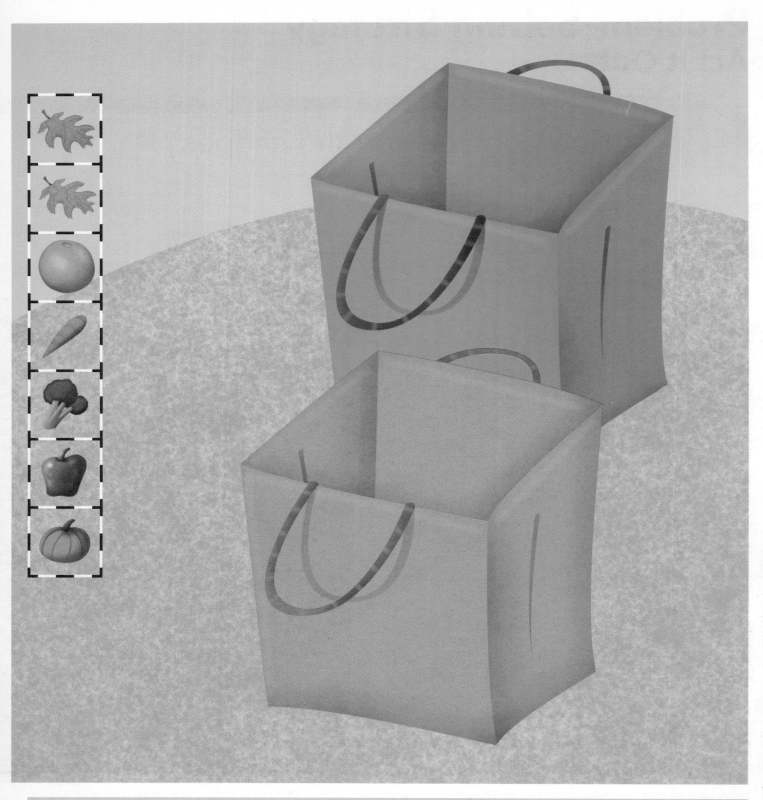

Directions: Cut out the objects. Sort the objects by color. Glue green objects in the green bag. Glue orange objects in the orange bag.

Math at Home Activity: Take advantage of problem-solving opportunities during daily routines such as riding in the car, bedtime, doing laundry, putting away groceries, planning schedules, and so on.

Sort by More Than One Attribute

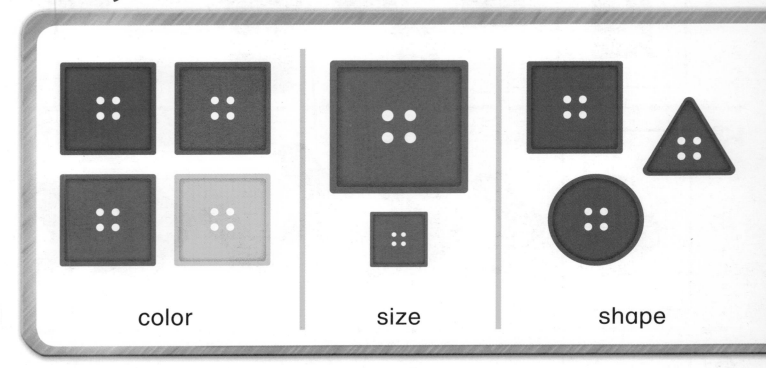

| color | size | shape |

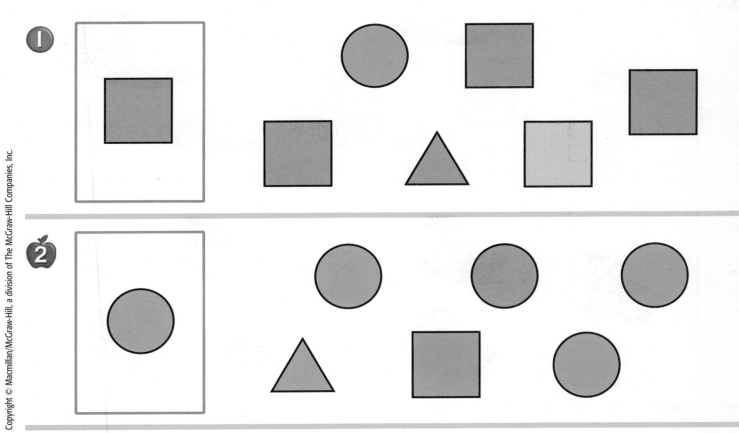

Directions:

1–2. Describe the colored figure in the box. Circle the figures in the group that are alike. Put an X on the figures that are not alike. Tell how you know.

Chapter 1   Lesson 4

twenty-three   **23**

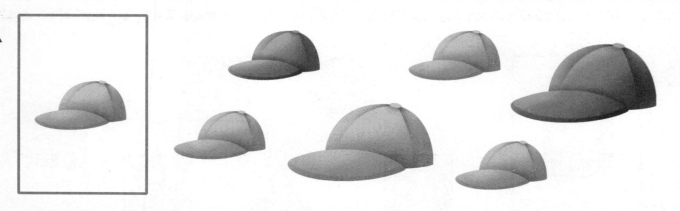

Directions:

3–6. Describe the size and color of the object in the box. Circle the objects that are alike. Put an X on the objects that are not alike. Tell how you know.

Math at Home Activity: Using shoes from all family members ask your child to sort the shoes into groups such as small white shoes or large brown shoes.

Name

     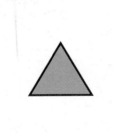

Directions:

1–2. Circle the objects that are alike. Mark an X on the objects that are different.

3. Sort the color tiles by drawing a line from each color tile to the same color bag.

4. Identify the colored figure in the box. Circle the figures in the group that are alike.
   Put an X on the figures that are not alike.

Chapter I

Button Up!

Sorting

You Will Need

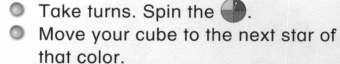
Play with a partner.
- Put your 🔲 on Start.
- Take turns. Spin the 🎡.
- Move your cube to the next star of that color.
- Take any figure or size attribute button that is this same color.
- First player to reach Finish wins!
- Find different ways to sort your buttons.

START

FINISH

Spin Again

Name _____

Same Number

Vocabulary

same number

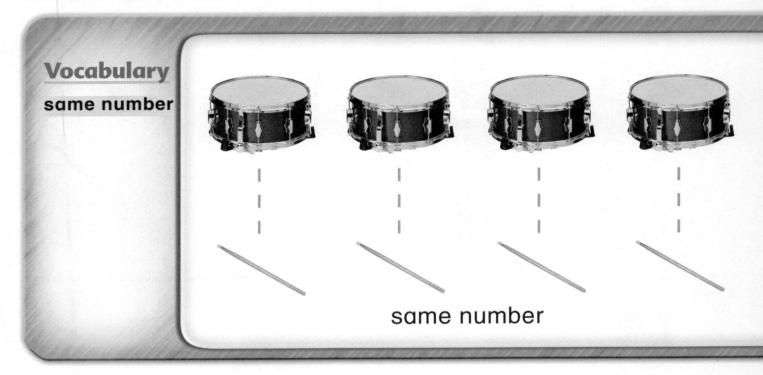

same number

①

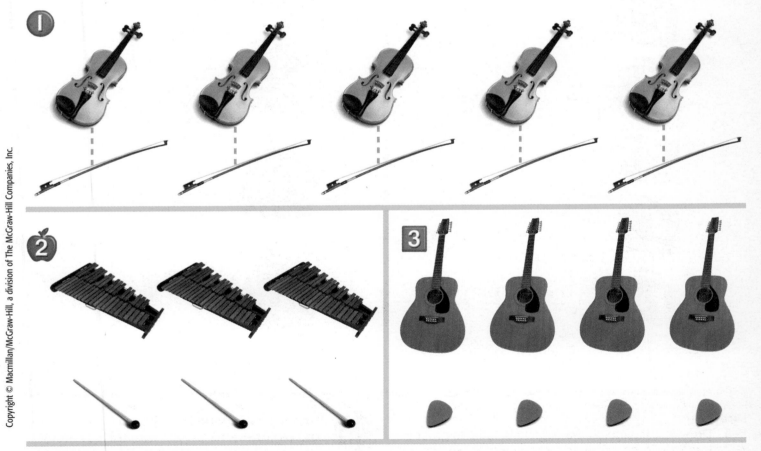

②

③

Directions:

1–3. Draw lines to match the objects in the two groups.
Describe the sizes of the two sets of objects.

Chapter 1   Lesson 5

4

5

6

7

Directions:

4–5. Draw lines to match the objects in the two groups.
6–7. Use color tiles to create a group that is the same number as the group of objects shown. Trace the color tiles. Draw lines to show that the groups have the same number.

Math at Home Activity: Gather four spoons, three pencils, and five pennies. Ask your child to gather the same number of objects. Match them to show the same number.

Name _____

More Than

Vocabulary

more than

more than

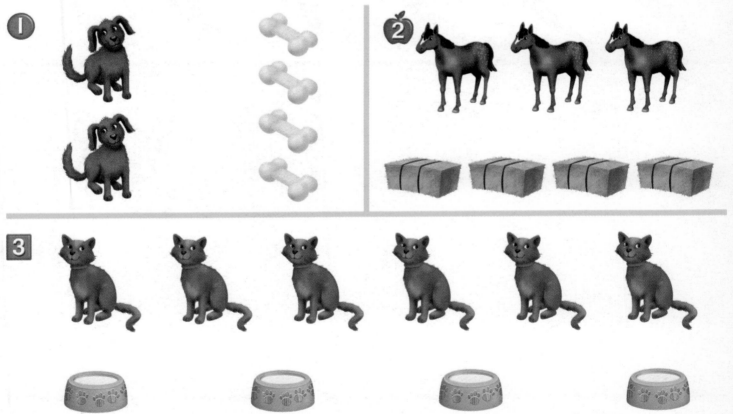

Directions:

1–3. Draw lines to match objects in the two groups.
Describe the sizes of the two sets of objects.
Circle the group that has more than the other group.

Chapter I   Lesson 6

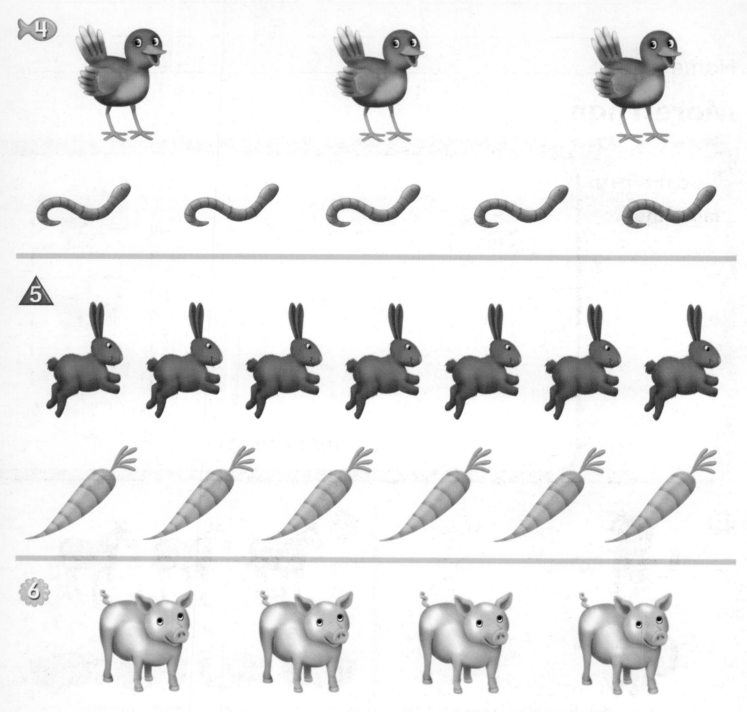

Directions:

4–5. Draw lines to match objects in the two groups.
Circle the group that has more than the other
group.

6. Use tiles to show a group with more tiles than pigs.
Trace the tiles.

 Math at Home Activity: Show 7 fingers. Have your
child show more fingers; fewer fingers.

Name _____

Less Than

Copyright © Macmillan/McGraw-Hill, a division of The McGraw-Hill Companies, Inc.

Vocabulary

less

less than

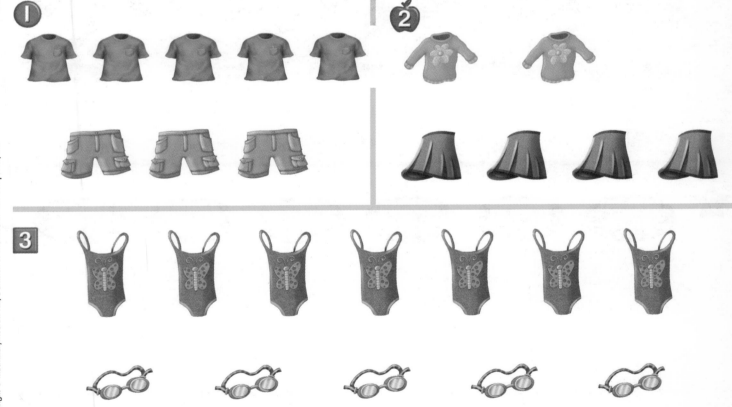

1

2

3

Directions:

1–3. Draw a line from an object in one group to match an object
in the other group. Circle the group that has two less.
Describe the sizes of the two sets of objects.

Chapter 1   Lesson 7

thirty-one **31**

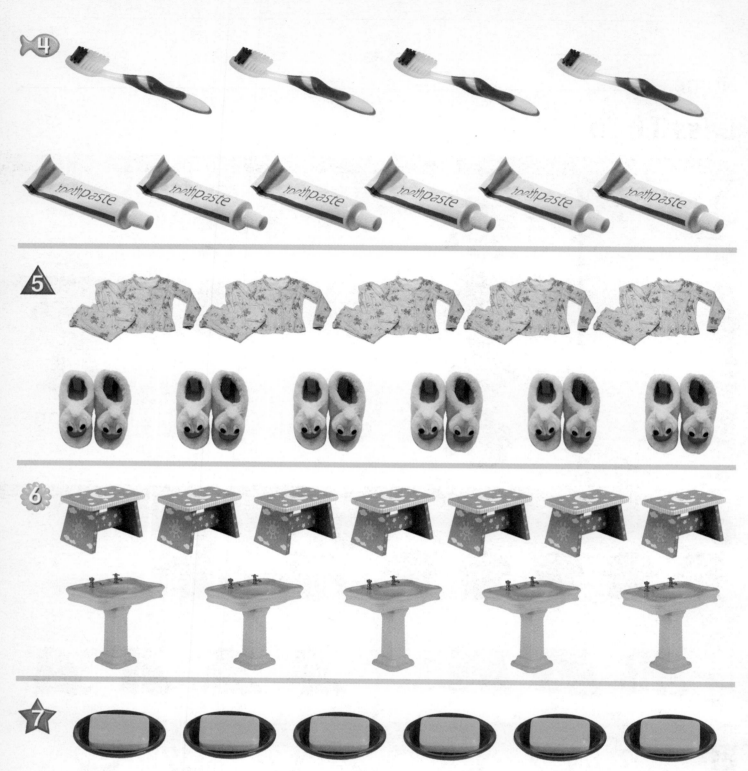

Directions:

4–6. Draw a line from an object in one group to match an object in the other group. Circle the group that has less objects.

7. Use tiles to show a group with less tiles than bars of soap. Trace the tiles.

Math at Home Activity: Gather three pencils and five crayons. Compare pencils and crayons. Discuss less than.

Chapter 1   Lesson 7

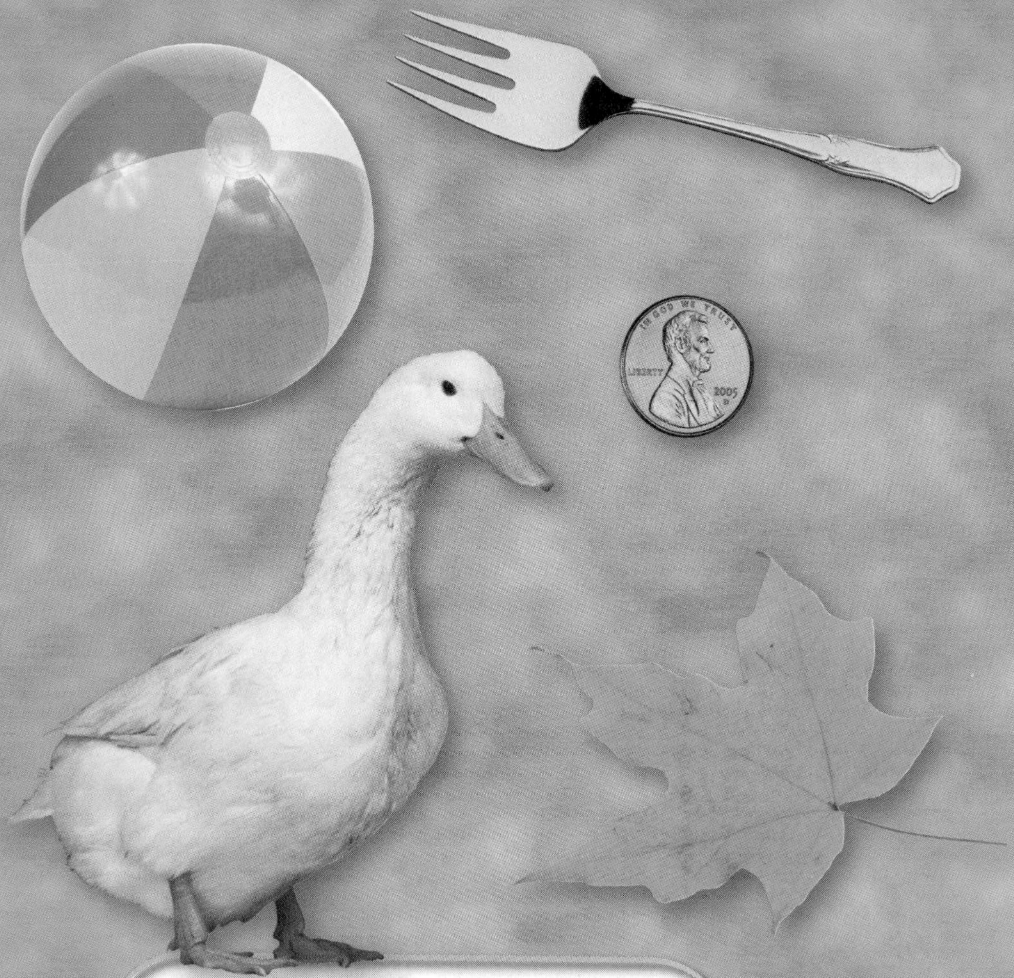

Circle the items that float. Put an X on the items that sink. Are there more that float or sink? Circle your answer.

Float Sink

LD DOWN

Problem Solving
in Science

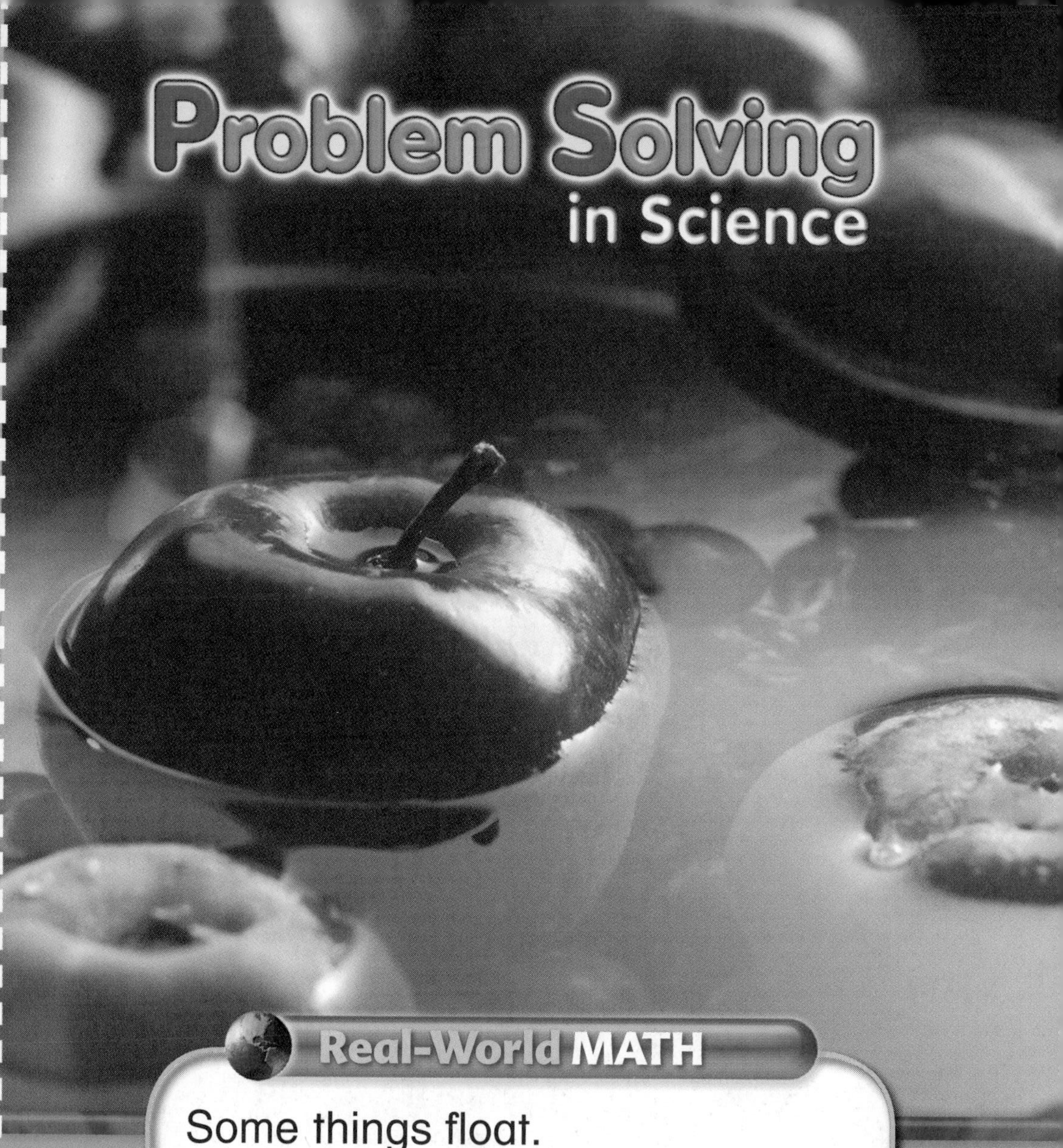

Real-World MATH

Some things float.
Some things sink.

This book belongs to

____

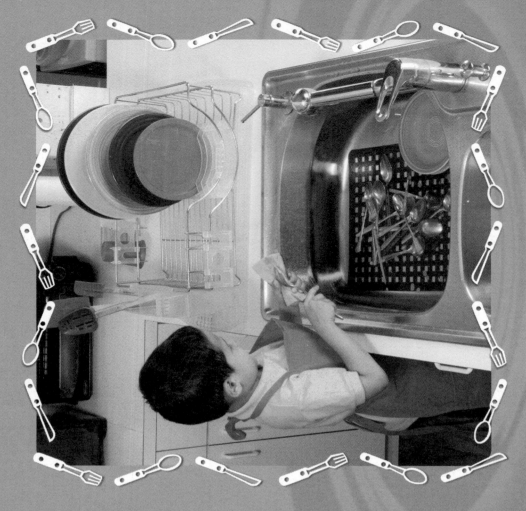

Silverware sinks.

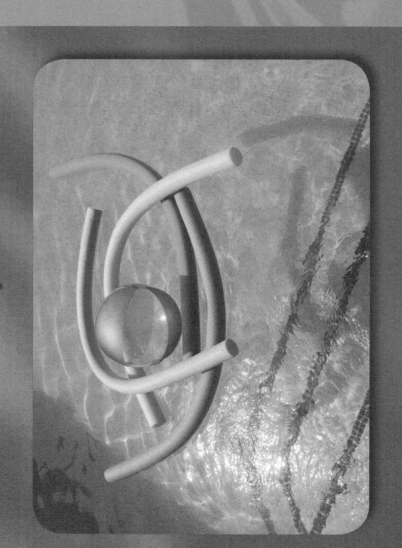

Some toys float.

Name _____

1

2

3

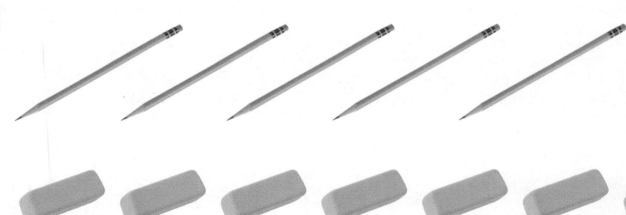

Directions:
1. Sort the cans by color. Draw a line from each soup can to where it belongs.
2. Draw a line from each object in one group to match an object in the other group.
3. Draw a line from each object in one group to match an object in the other group. Circle the group that has two less objects than the other group.

Chapter 1

Name _____

1

2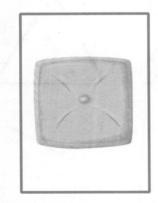

3

Directions:
1. Circle the objects that are alike. Mark an X on the one that
   is different.
2. Look at the pillow in the box. Circle the pillows that are alike.
   Mark an X on the pillows that are different.
3. Draw a line from each object in one group to match an object in the
   other group. Circle the group that shows more objects than the other group.

36   thirty-six

Name _____

A.

○   ○   ○

B.

○   ○   ○

1.

○   ○   ○

2.

○   ○   ○

Directions: Listen as your teacher reads the problem. Choose the best answer.

3.

○   ○   ○

4.

○   ○   ○

5.

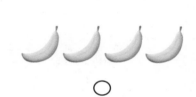

○   ○   ○

6.

○   ○   ○

Directions: Listen as your teacher reads the problem. Choose the best answer.

Summative Assessment

Use Numbers 0 to 5

Copyright © Macmillan/McGraw-Hill, a division of The McGraw-Hill Companies, Inc.

**Key
Vocabulary**

count

number

order

Explore

How many raccoons?

How many noses?

Name _____

Are You Ready for Chapter 2?

1

2

3

4

Directions:

1. Match each cat to one cat bed by drawing a line.
2. Color 3 apples.
3. Look at the picture. Count the flowers. Draw that many flowers.
4. Look at the picture. Count the baseballs. Draw that many baseballs.

40 forty

This page checks skills needed for Chapter 2.

Dear Family,

Today my class started Chapter 2, **Use Numbers 0 to 5.** I will learn to count and compare numbers zero to five. Here are my vocabulary words, an activity we can do, and a list of books we can read together.

Love,

_____

Activity

Ask your child to count different objects. For example, ask how many pillows are on the bed, how many plates are on the table, or how many cans are in the cupboard.

Key Vocabulary

count
          1   2   3

order 1, 3, 6, 7, 9
these numbers are in order from smallest to largest

Math Online Click on the eGlossary link at tx.grKmath.com to find out more about these words. There are 13 languages.

Books to Read

One, Two, Three, How Many Animals Can You See?
by Emilie Boon
Orchard Books, 1996.

I, 2, 3 To the Zoo
by Eric Carle
Putnam, 1998.

At the Edge of the Woods: A Counting Book
by Cynthia Cotten
Henry Holt and Co., 2002.

Estimada Familia,

Hoy mi clase comenzó el Capítulo 2, **Usa los números desde el 0 hasta el 5**. Aprenderé a contar y a comparar los números del cero al cinco. A continuación, están mis palabras de vocabulario, una actividad que podemos realizar y una lista de libros que podemos leer juntos.

Cariños, _____

Actividad

Pídanle a su hijo(a) que cuente diferentes objetos. Por ejemplo, pregúntenle cuántas almohadas hay en la cama, cuántos platos hay en la mesa o cuántas latas hay en la alacena.

Vocabulario clave

contar
1   2   3

ordenar   1, 3, 6, 7, 9
estos números están en order del menor al mayor

Math Online Visiten el enlace eGlossary en tx.grKmath.com para averiguar más sobre estas palabras, las cuales se muestran en 13 idiomas

Libros recomendados

Los cinco patitos
de Pam Paparone
North South Books, 2007.

1, 2, 3, Gatitos
de Michael Van Zeveren
Ekaré Express, 2006.

Name _____

Numbers 1, 2, and 3

Vocabulary

count

one

two

three

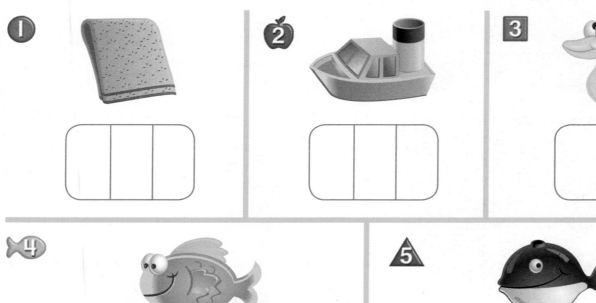

Directions:

1–5. Identify the object. Use the picture above to count how many of that object. Use color tiles to show that many of each object. Color one box for each object counted. Say that number.

6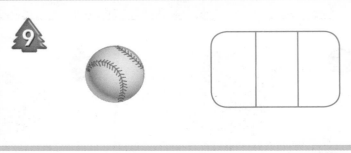

7

8

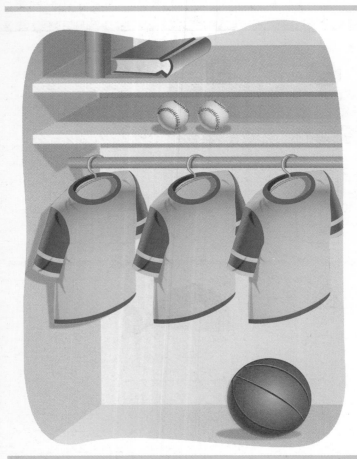

9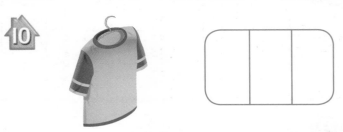

10

11

Directions:

6–11. Identify the object. Use the picture to count how many of that object. Use color tiles to show that many of each object. Color one box for each object counted. Say that number.

Math at Home Activity: Gather items such as paper clips, rubber bands, or sheets of paper. Put them in groups of one, two, and three. Practice counting the items in each group.

44 forty-four

Chapter 2   Lesson 1

Name _____

Read and Write 1, 2, and 3

Vocabulary

number

①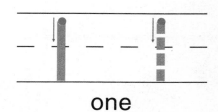
one

②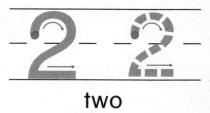
two

③
three

Directions:
1. Draw one butterfly. Trace the number 1.
2. Draw two baseballs. Trace the number 2.
3. Draw three flowers. Trace the number 3.

Chapter 2   Lesson 2

4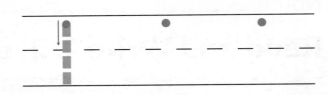

5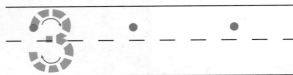

6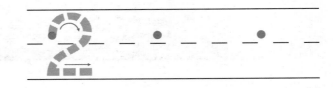

7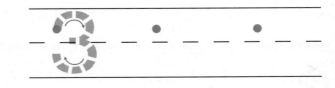

8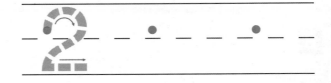

Directions:

4–8. Count the objects in each row. Say the
number. Write that number three times.

 Math at Home Activity: Show your child 3 spoons, 2 cups,
and 1 bowl. Count how many of each. Write that number.

Chapter 2   Lesson 2

Name _____

Numbers 4 and 5

Vocabulary

four
five

4
four

5
five

1

2

Directions:
1. Draw 5 berries on the bush.
2. Cut and glue 4 berries on the bush.

Directions: Count each group of bees. Say the number. Circle each group of four bees. Place an X on each group of five bees.

Math at Home Activity: Help your child gather objects such as pennies, cups, or toy figures. Put objects in groups of four and groups of five. Practice counting the objects in each group.

Name _____

Read and Write 4 and 5

 1

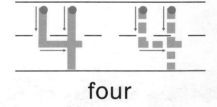

four

 2

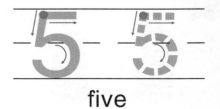

five

Directions:
1. Draw four cones. Trace the number 4.
2. Draw five bricks. Trace the number 5.

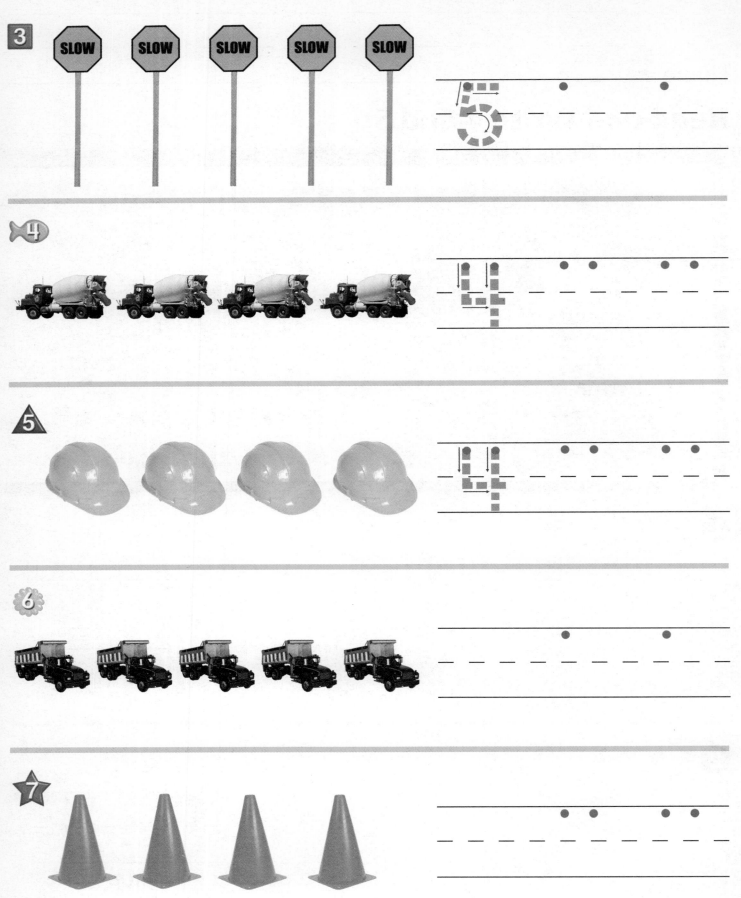

3 SLOW SLOW SLOW SLOW SLOW

5

4

5

6

7

Directions:
3–7. Count the objects in each row. Say the number. Write the numbers.

 Math at Home Activity: Make groups of 4 and 5 using cereal or macaroni. Have your child count how many in each group and write that number.

Name _____

①

_____
_ _ _ _ _
_____

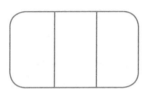

②

③

_____
_ _ _ _ _
_____

Directions:
1. Count each object. Color a box for each object counted. Write the number.
2. Circle each group of five frogs. Place an X on each group of four frogs.
3. Count the objects. Write the number.

Game Time

Rainbow Crossing
Counting

You Will Need

10 ◯

▦ 5

Play with a partner. Take turns.
- ◯ Roll the ▦5 .
- ◯ Move your cube that number of spaces.
- ◯ If you land on:

Red—take 1 ◯

Blue—put 1 ◯ back

Yellow—wait until next turn
- ◯ When both players reach finish, count to see who has more ◯ .

START ▶

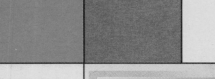

FINISH ▶

Name _____

Problem-Solving Strategy
Draw a Picture

How Many Ducks?

Draw

Directions: Draw a line from the ring at the end of each fishing
line to a duck. Draw a circle for each duck that was caught. Explain
your drawing. Tell how many ducks were caught.

How Many Ducks?

Directions: Each child caught one duck. Draw a line from each child's pole to the duck that was caught. Draw one circle for each duck that was not caught. Tell how many ducks were not caught.

 Math at Home Activity: Take advantage of problem-solving opportunities during daily routines such as going to the grocery store. Have your child help you make the grocery list by drawing pictures of the grocery items needed.

Read and Write 0

Vocabulary

zero

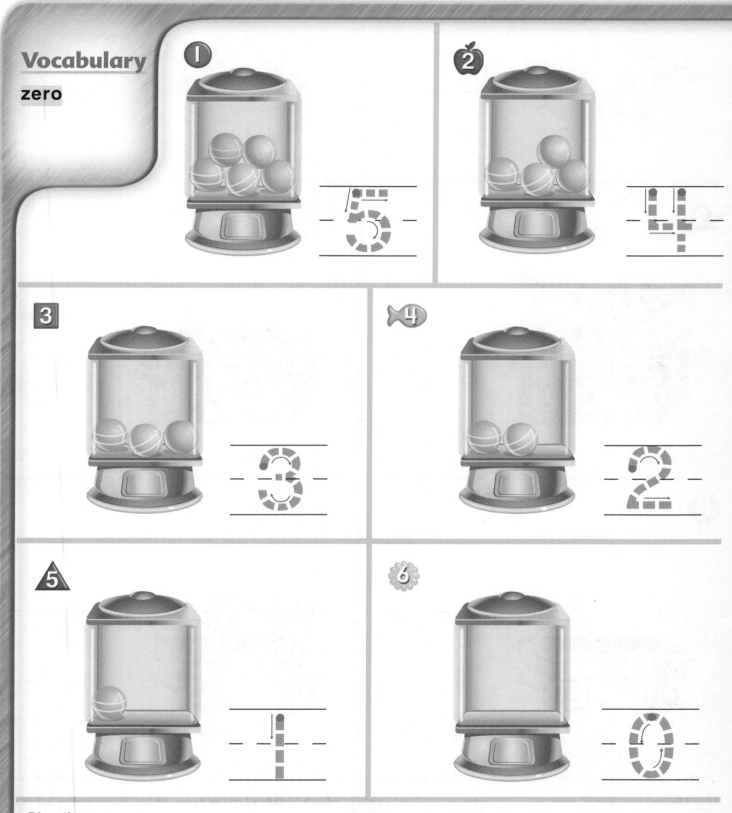

1 5

2 4

3 3

4 2

5 1

6 0

Directions:

1–6. Count how many balls in each machine. Say the number. Write the number that shows how many.

Directions:

7–8. Write how many fish are in the fish bowl.

9–10. Write how many cats are in the box.

11–12. Write how many puppies are in the wagon.

Math at Home Activity: Look at a family photo. Ask your child questions that will give zero as the answer. Practice writing the number zero with your child.

56   fifty-six

Name _____

Compare Numbers 0 to 5

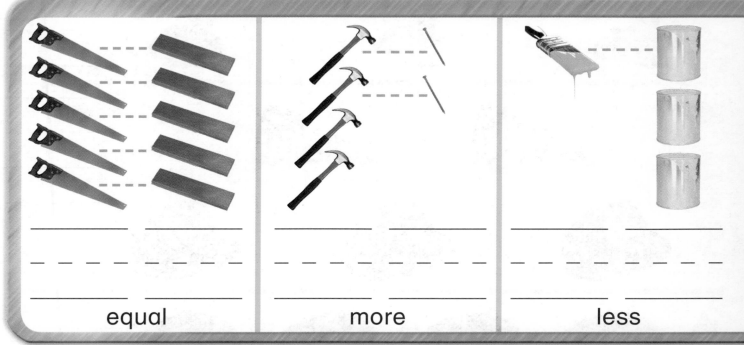

equal | more | less

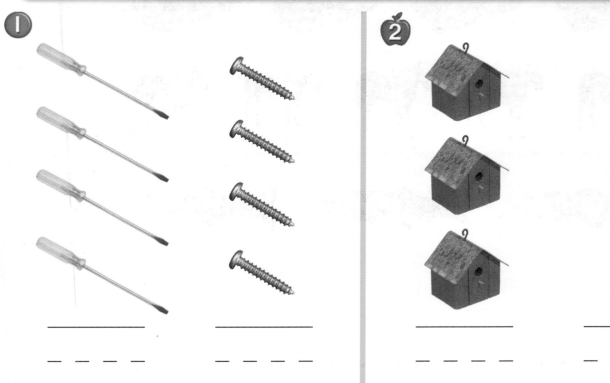

Directions:
1–2. Draw lines to match the objects in one group with objects in the other. Write the number in each group. Put an X on the group and number that has more. Put a circle around the group and number that has less. Draw a box around the groups and numbers that are equal.

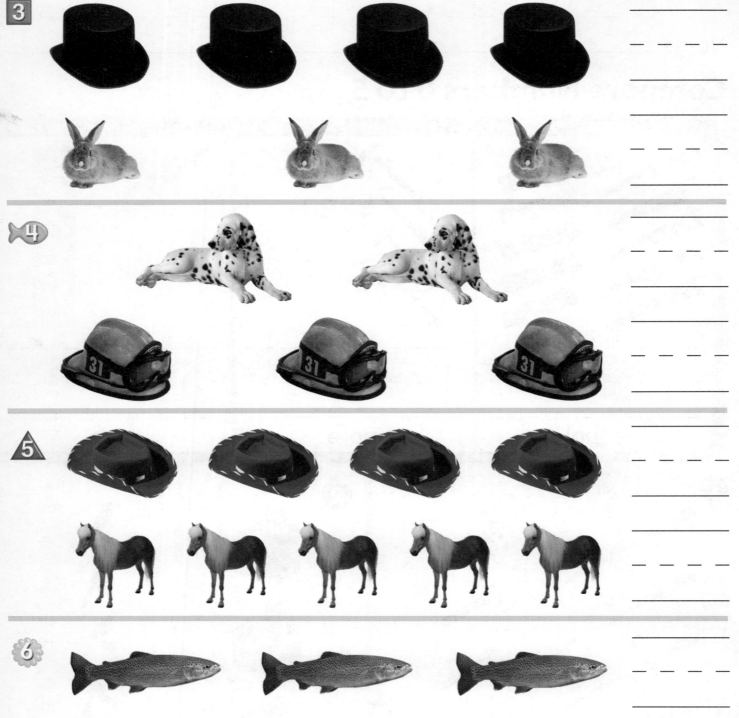

3 _____

4 _____

5 _____

6 _____

Directions:

3–4. Draw lines to match the objects in each row. Write the number. Put an X on the group and number that has more.

5. Draw a line to match the objects in each row. Write the number. Circle the group and number that has less.

6. Draw a group that has less. Write the number in each group.

Math at Home Activity: Make two groups of toys or books, up to 5 items, in each group. Ask your child which group has more, which has less, or is equal. Write the numbers. Practice with other groupings.

Chapter 2 Lesson 7

Order Numbers 0 to 5

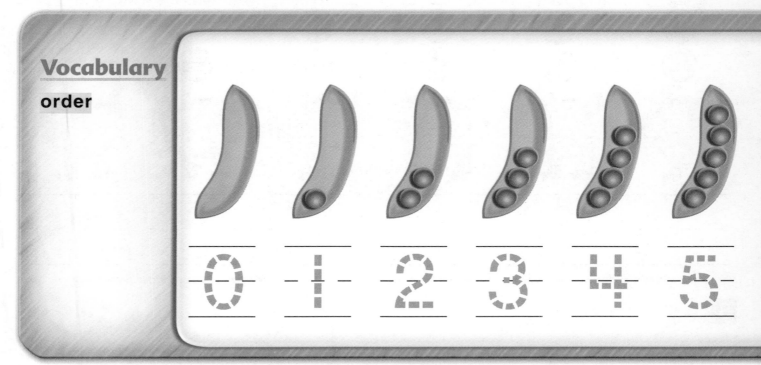

1

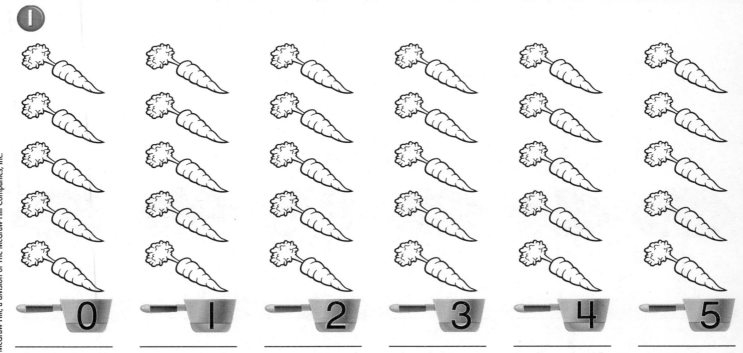

Directions:

1. Identify the number. Color that number of carrots.
   Write the numbers in order from 0 to 5.

②
_____ _____ _____ _____ _____ _____

---

③
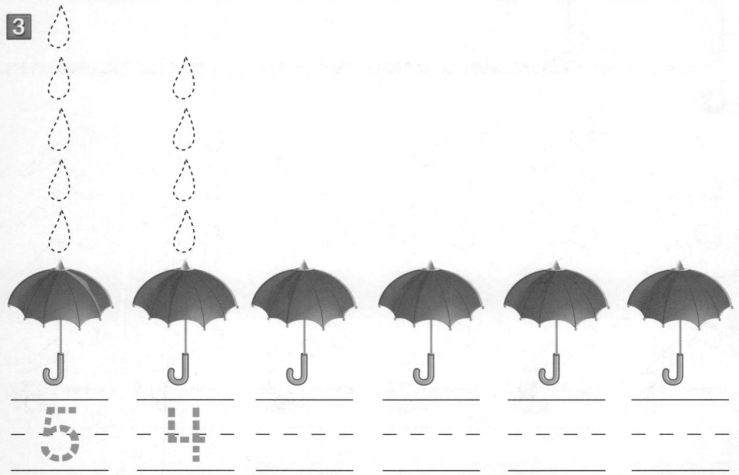

5   4

Directions:

2. Count the pennies going into each bank. Write the number on the line.

3. Identify the number. Trace it. Trace that many raindrops. Write the remaining numbers in order and draw the raindrops to show how many.

Math at Home Activity: Write numbers 0 through 5 on paper. Use one paper per number. Find objects to place on the sheets of paper to show that number. Talk about order of numbers.

D

How many people do you see?

——— people

A

Problem Solving
in Social Studies

Real-World MATH

It is early. The store is closed.
How many people do you see?

——— people

This book belongs to

———

Here is the baker.

How many people want to buy bread?

—— people

Here is a store worker.

How many people do you see?

—— person

C

B

Name _____

1

_____

— — — —

_____

2

_____

— — — —

_____

_____

— — — —

_____

3

| 0 | 1 | 2 | 3 | 4 | 5 |

_____

— — — —

_____

Directions:
1. Write how many fish are in the fish bowl.
2. Draw a line from each object in one row to an object in the row below.
   Count the objects in each row. Write the number. Put an X on the
   group and number that is more.
3. Identify the number. Color the number of basketballs shown on the hoop.
   Write the numbers in order from 0 to 5.

Chapter 2

Name _____

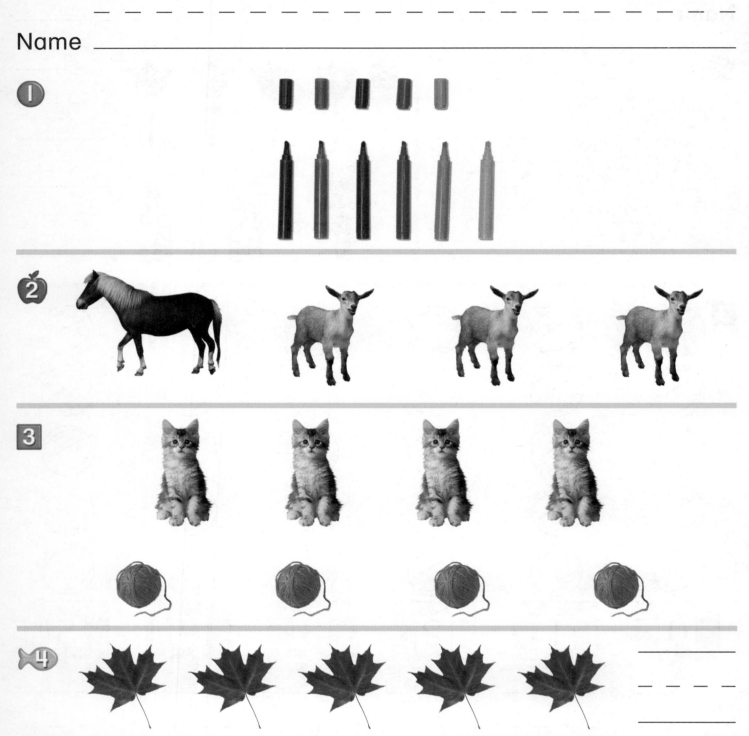

①

②

③

④

Directions:

1. Draw a line from each object in one group to match an object in the other group. Circle the group that has less.
2. Circle the objects that are the same. Mark an X on the objects that are different.
3. Draw a line from each object in one group to match an object in the other group.
4. Count the objects. Write the number.

Name _____

A.

○   ○   ○

B.

4   5   6

○   ○   ○

1.

3

2   4   5

○   ○   ○

2.

○   ○   ○

Directions: Listen as the teacher reads the problem.
Choose the best answer.

3.

      ○   ○   ○

4.

      ○   ○   ○

5.

1   2   0

○   ○   ○

6.

2   3   4

○   ○   ○

Directions: Listen as the teacher reads the problem.
Choose the best answer.

Summative Assessment

Describe Position and Patterns

Key Vocabulary

top

middle

bottom

pattern

Explore

What colors are the stripes on the zebra's face?

Are You Ready for Chapter 3?

1

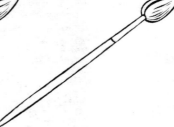 

2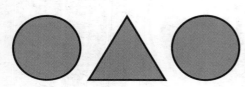

3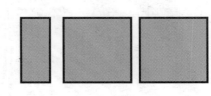

4

Directions:

1. Color the first paintbrush yellow, the second blue, the third red, and the fourth green. Draw a line to match each brush to the same color paint.

2–3. Circle the figure that is different.

4. Copy the figures by drawing them in the space below.

Dear Family,

Today my class started Chapter 3, **Describe Position and Patterns**. I will be learning about position words and how to find and create patterns using objects, sounds, and movements. Here are my vocabulary words, an activity we can do, and a list of books we can read together.

Love,

_____

Activity

Make up clap, slap, stomp patterns and have your child copy them. Repeat each pattern 3 times. When your child can repeat your patterns, switch.

Key Vocabulary

top

middle

bottom

pattern

pattern unit

Math Online Click on the eGlossary link at tx.grKmath.com to find out more about this word. There are 13 languages.

Books to Read

Five Little Monkeys Jumping on the Bed
by Eileen Christelow
Clarion Books, 1998.

Jump, Frog, Jump
by Robert Kalan
Harper Collins
Publishers, 1989.

Pattern Fish
by Trudy Harris
Lerner Publishing
Group, 2000.

Estimada familia:

Hoy mi clase comenzó el Capítulo 3, **Describe posiciones y patrones**. Aprenderé acerca de palabras que tengan que ver con posición y a encontrar y hacer patrones con colores tamaños y formas. A continuación, están mis palabras de vocabulario, una actividad que podemos realizar y una lista de libros que podemos leer juntos.

Cariños,

_____

Actividad

Inventen patrones de aplausos, palmadas y pisadas fuertes y pídanle a su hijo(a) que los repita. Repitan 3 veces cada patrón. Cuando su hijo(a) repita fácilmente sus patrones, cámbienlos.

Vocabulario clave

arriba

medio

abajo

patrón

patrón
unitario

Math Online Visiten el enlace eGlossary en tx.grKmath.com para averiguar más sobre estas palabras, las cuales se muestran en 13 idiomas.

Libros recomendados

Cinco monitos brincando en la cama
de Eileen Christelow
Clarion Books, 2005.

¡Salta, Ranita, Salta!
de Robert Kalan
Live Oak Media, 2005

¿Patrones: Que hay en la pared?
de John Burstein
Gareth Stevens
Publishing, 2006

Name _____

Over and Under

Vocabulary

over

above

under

below

Directions:

1. Describe the position of each banana using the words over, under, above, or below. Circle the bananas that are over or above a monkey. Underline bananas that are under or below a monkey.

2. Place a yellow color tile over or above each monkey. Draw a banana where you placed each color tile.

Chapter 3   Lesson 1   seventy-one   **71**

3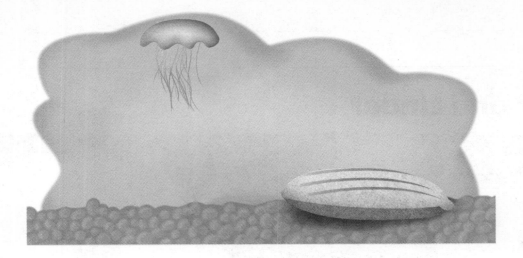

5

Directions:

3–4. Place a blue color tile above the object.
Place a yellow color tile below the object.
Draw a fish where you placed each color tile.

5. Describe the position of each fish using the
words over, under, above, or below. Circle the
fish that is above or over. Put an X on the fish
that is under or below.

Math at Home Activity: When cleaning up at home give
your child directions using the words above, below, over, and
under. For example: Put your shoes on the floor below the coats
in the closet. Stack these books above the games on the shelf.

Chapter 3 Lesson 1

Name _____

Top, Middle, Bottom

Vocabulary

top

middle

bottom

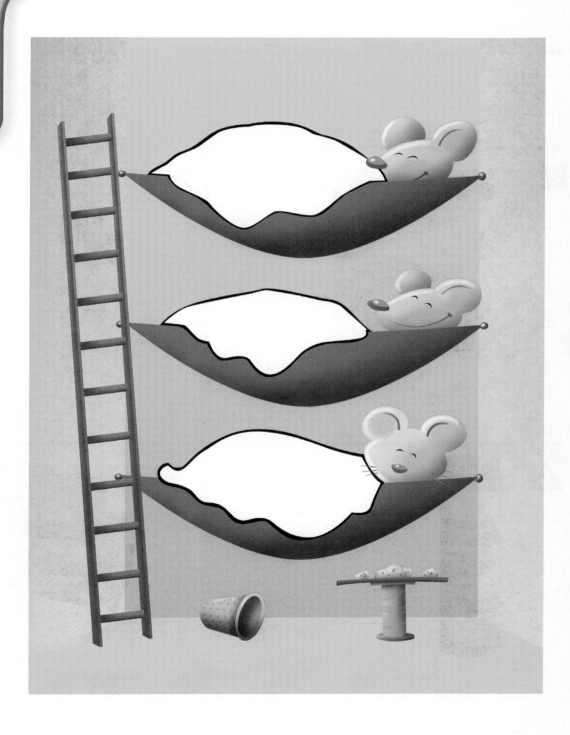

Directions: Place a red color tile on the bottom blanket. Place a
yellow color tile on the middle blanket. Place a green tile on the
top blanket. Color the blankets to match the color tiles.

1

2

3

 4

5

6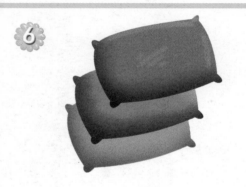

Directions:
1–2. Put an X on the object on top.
3–4. Circle the object on the bottom.
5–6. Put an X on the object in the middle.

Math at Home Activity: Play "I Spy" with your child. Have him or her find things that are on top, in the middle, or on the bottom of something else. Use those words in your description of the object.

Objects: Before and After

Vocabulary

before

after

①

②

Directions:
1. Place a color tile on the rooster that is before the chick. Trace the color tile.
2. Is the duck before or after the frog? Circle the animal that is before the frog.

3

4

5

6

Directions:

3–4. Place a yellow color tile on the animal that is before the other animals. Circle it. Place a blue color tile on the animal that is after the other animals. Put an X on the animal.

5. Is the blue bird before or after the red bird? Circle the blue bird.

6. Is the brown horse before or after the white horse? Circle the brown horse.

Math at Home Activity: Have your child help you make dinner. Ask him or her what you will need to do before you start cooking or what you will need to do after you are done eating. After you eat, ask your child questions about what you did together using the words before and after.

Chapter 3   Lesson 3

Identifying Patterns

Vocabulary

pattern

①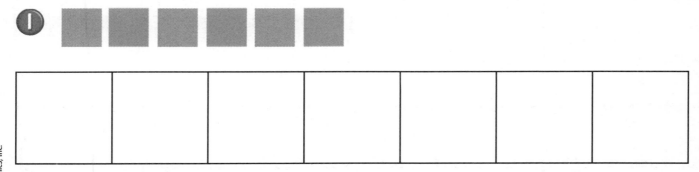

②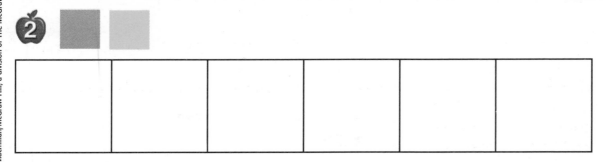

Directions:

1. Identify the pattern. Use color tiles to copy and extend the pattern. Color the boxes to show the pattern.

2. Use color tiles to create your own pattern using the two tile colors shown. Color the boxes to show the pattern you created. Explain your pattern.

3

4

5

6

Directions:

3. Identify the pattern. Use color tiles to create and extend the pattern. Color the boxes to show the pattern.

4. Create your own pattern using the two tile colors shown. Color the boxes to show your pattern.

5–6. Use two colors to create your own pattern using color tiles. Color the boxes to show the pattern you created. Explain your pattern.

Math at Home Activity: Have your child find something in your home that represents an AB pattern.

Name _____

1

2

3

4

Directions:
1. Circle the balloon that is above the tree.
2. Underline the bird on the middle branch. Put an X on the bird on the top branch.
3. Circle the car that is before the red truck. Put an X on the car that is after the green car.
4. Underline the object that could come next in the pattern.

Chapter 3

seventy-nine 79

Pattern Strings

Patterning

Play with a partner.
- Take a string. Choose a pattern.
- Roll .
- Move your cube that many spaces.
- If you land on the color that comes next in your pattern, add the correct button to your string. If not, wait for your next turn.
- The first person to finish their pattern string is the winner.

You Will Need

2

Start →

Object Patterns

1

2

Directions:

1–2. Identify the pattern. Use attribute buttons to create the pattern.
Circle the button that could come next in the pattern. Explain.

Chapter 3   Lesson 5

3

4

5

6

Directions:

3–5. Use attribute buttons to create the pattern. Circle the button that could come next in the pattern. Explain.

6. Use the buttons shown to create your own pattern. Color the boxes to show your pattern another way.

Math at Home Activity: Have your child use canned goods and boxes of food to create his or her own pattern. Ask him or her to explain the pattern by telling you why they put the objects in a certain order.

Name _____

Problem-Solving Strategy
Look for a Pattern

Can you show this another way?

1

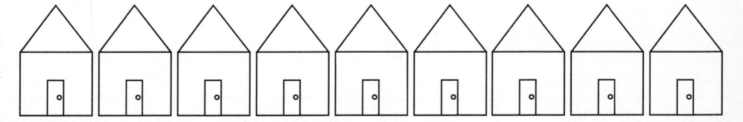

Directions:

1. Look at each row. Identify the pattern. Create the pattern another way using color tiles. Color the houses to show the pattern. Explain your pattern.

Chapter 3   Lesson 6

eighty-three **83**

Directions:
2. Look at each row. Identify the pattern. Create the pattern another way using color tiles. Color the stars to show the pattern. Explain your pattern.
3. Look at the pictures in the row. Identify the pattern. Draw shapes to create a pattern to match. Explain your pattern.

Math at Home Activity: Take advantage of problem-solving opportunities during daily routines such as riding in the car, bedtime, doing laundry, putting away groceries, planning schedules, and so on.

84   eighty-four

Chapter 3   Lesson 6

Name _____

Sound Patterns

1

2

3

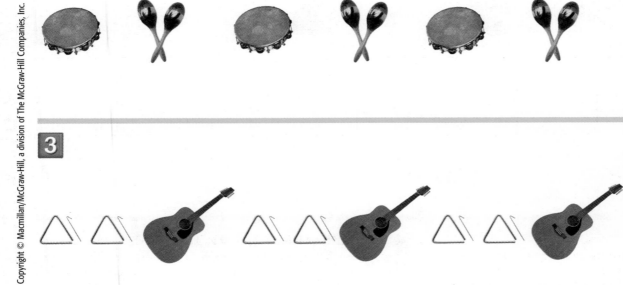

Directions:
1–3. Identify the pattern. Extend the pattern by circling the instrument
that makes the sound that could come next.

Chapter 3   Lesson 7

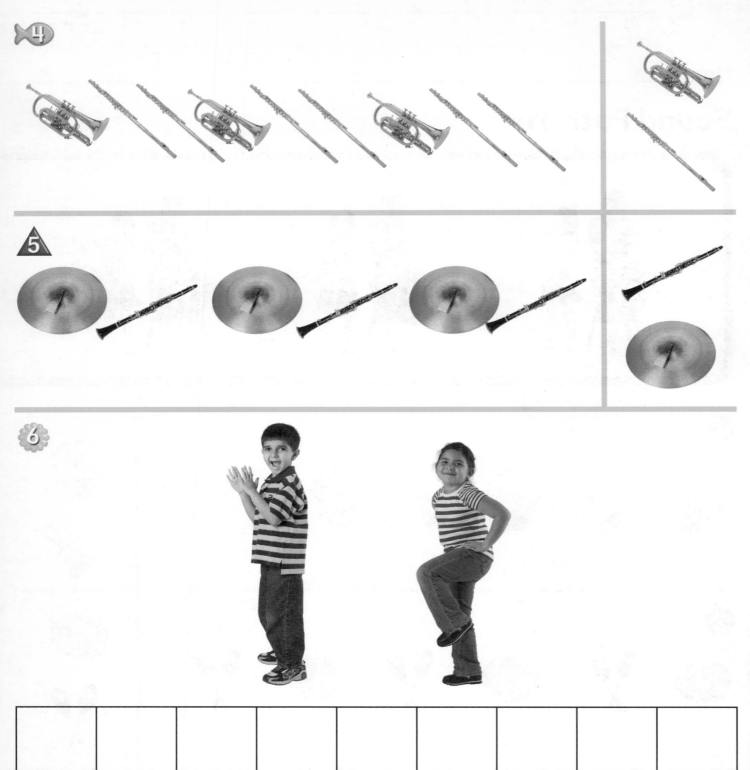

Directions:

4–5. Extend the pattern by circling the instrument that makes the sound that could come next.

6. Create a sound pattern using the sounds shown. Show your pattern another way in the squares.

Math at Home Activity: Have your child create different sound patterns using a wooden or plastic spoon, different size pots, and plastic containers. Have him or her create an AB, ABB, and AAB pattern by hitting the pots and containers with the spoon.

Name _____

Physical Movement Patterns

1

2

Directions:

1–2. Identify the pattern. Extend the pattern by circling the movement that could come next.

Chapter 3   Lesson 8

3

4

5

6

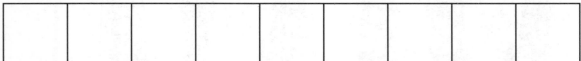

Directions:

3–5. Extend the pattern by circling the movement that could come next.

6. Create a movement pattern. Show your pattern another way in the squares. Explain your pattern by acting it out.

 Math at Home Activity: Create movement patterns and have your child copy your pattern. Then allow your child to make up his or her own pattern and watch to see if you can copy it correctly. Be sure to try AB, ABB, AAB patterns.

Chapter 3   Lesson 8

Predicting Patterns

When it is you need  .

When it is you need  .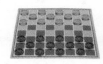

---

①

When it is you wear  .

When it is you wear  .

---

②

When it is you play .

When it is you play  .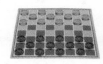

Directions:
1. If the weather pattern continues what will you wear tomorrow? Circle it.
2. If the weather pattern continues what will you play tomorrow? Circle it.

If then .

If then .

 4

If then  .

If then .

5

If then .

If then .

Directions:

3–5. Every day Sam and Kim flip a counter to help them decide what to play. Each color stands for a different activity each day. If each pattern continues, what activity will they do next. Circle it.

Chapter 3   Lesson 9

A pattern is on the plate. What pattern do you see?

Color the boxes to show the pattern another way. Explain.

☐ ☐ ☐ ☐ ☐ ☐

Problem Solving
in Art

Real-World MATH

Patterns are everywhere! Let's look in the kitchen.

This book belongs to

_____

Is there a pattern on me?

Patterns are on the cup.
What pattern do you see?

Patterns are on the table.
What patterns do you see?

C

B

Name _____

①

②

③

FINISH

④

⑤

Directions:
1. Circle the bug that is above the branch. Put an X on the bug that is under the branch.
2. Circle the box that is on top. Put an X on the box that is in the middle. Underline the box that is on the bottom.
3. Circle the boat that is before the red boat. Put an X on the boat that is after the green boat.
4–5. Circle the picture that shows what could come next.

Chapter 3

Summative Assessment

Name _____

1

2

3

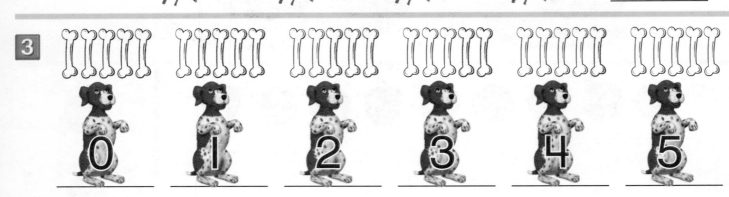

0   1   2   3   4   5

4

Directions:

1. Circle the shapes that are alike. Put an X on the shapes that are different.
2. Draw a line from each object in one row to an object in the row below. Count the objects in each row. Write the number. Put an X on the number and group that is more.
3. Color the number of bones. Write the numbers in order from 0 to 5.
4. Count the animals. Write the number.

Formative Assessment

Name _____

A.

above
○

below
○

next to
○

B.

○

○

○

1.

○

○

○

2.

○

○

○

Directions: Listen as your teacher reads the problem.
Choose the best answer.

Chapter 3

3.

○ ○ ○

4.

○ ○ ○

5.

4 5 6

○ ○ ○

6.

○ ○ ○

Directions: Listen as your teacher reads the problem.
Choose the best answer.

Summative Assessment

CHAPTER 4

Use Numbers to 10

Key Vocabulary

ordinal numbers

Explore

How many eggs do you see?

Name _____

①

②

③

④

_____   _____

_ _ _ _ _ _ _   _ _ _ _ _ _ _

_____

Directions:
1. Draw a line from each baseball to a baseball mitt.
2. Color 5 leaves green.
3. Circle the row with 4 nests.
4. Count the objects in each group. Write the number.
   Draw a circle around the group that has more.

98   ninety-eight

Dear Family,

Today my class started Chapter 4, **Use Numbers to 10**. I will be learning to count and order numbers to 10. Here are my vocabulary words, an activity we can do, and a list of books we can read together.

Love,

_____

Activity

Count the types of clothes in a closet. You write the word and your child can write the number of items.

Key Vocabulary

ordinal numbers

first   second   third

Math Online Click on the eGlossary link at tx.grKmath.com to find out more about these words. There are 13 languages.

Books to Read

Ten Flashing Fireflies
by Philemon Sturges
North-South Books,
1995.

Mouse Count
by Ellen Stoll Walsh
Voyager Books,
1995.

I Hunter
by Pat Hutchins,
Harper Collins
Publishers, 1986.

Estimada familia:

Hoy mi clase comenzó el Capítulo 4, **Usa los números hasta el 10**. A continuación, están mis palabras de vocabulario, una actividad que podemos realizar y una lista de libros que podemos leer juntos.

Cariños, _____

Actividad

Cuenten los tipos de ropa que hay en el armario. Ustedes escriben la palabra y su hijo(a) escribe el número de artículos.

Vocabulario clave

Números ordinales

primero   segundo   tercero

Math Online Visiten el enlace eGlossary en tx.grKmath.com para averiguar más sobre estas palabras, las cuales se muestran en 13 idiomas

Libros recomendados

¿Cómo cuentan hasta diez los dinosaurios?
de Jane Yolan and Mark Teague
Scholastic, 2004.

Cuenta ratones
de Ellen Stoll Walsh
Fondo de Cultura Economica
USA, 1996.

Uno, dos, tres
de Pat Mora,
Clarion Books, 2000.

Name _____

Numbers 6 and 7

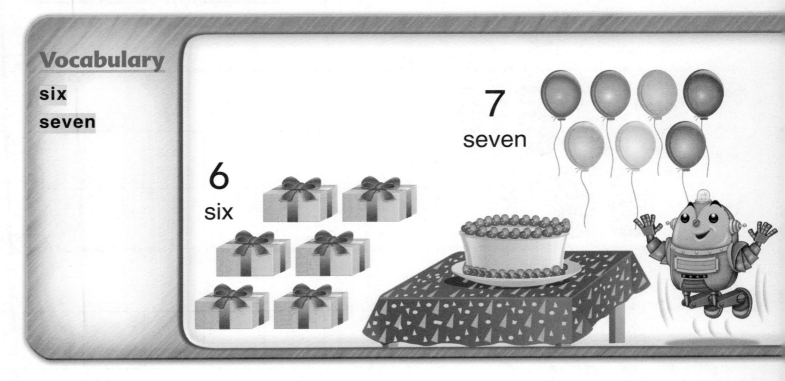

Vocabulary

six

seven

6
six

7
seven

1

2

Directions:

1. Count the objects in the row. Say the number. Use color tiles to show how many objects. Draw a box around each bow.
2. Count the objects in the row. Say the number. Use color tiles to show how many objects. Draw a string for each balloon.

3
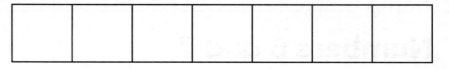

4

5
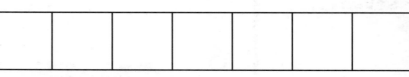

6
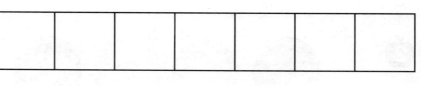

7
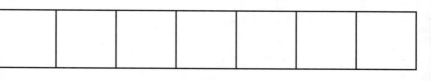

Directions:

3–7. Use color tiles to count the objects in each group. Say the number. Count and color one box for each object in that group.

 Math at Home Activity: Take a walk with your child. Find six and seven objects such as mailboxes or houses. Have your child count the objects.

Chapter 4   Lesson 1

Name _____

Number 8

Copyright © Macmillan/McGraw-Hill, a division of The McGraw-Hill Companies, Inc.

Vocabulary

eight

8 eight

Directions: Count the insects in each group. Use cubes to show how many insects.
Circle the groups of insects that show eight. Put an X on the groups that do not show eight.
Tell a classmate how many insects there are in each group.

Chapter 4   Lesson 2

one hundred three

_____

- - - - - - - - -

_____

_____

- - - - - - - - -

_____

_____

- - - - - - - - -

_____

_____

- - - - - - - - -

_____

Directions:

4–7. Count the objects in each row. Say the number. Use WorkMat 5 and counters to show the number. Write the number.

Math at Home Activity: Using six index cards help your child make 2 cards with 6 dots, 7 dots, and 8 dots. Write each number. Play a matching game.

Chapter 4   Lesson 3

Number 8

Vocabulary

eight

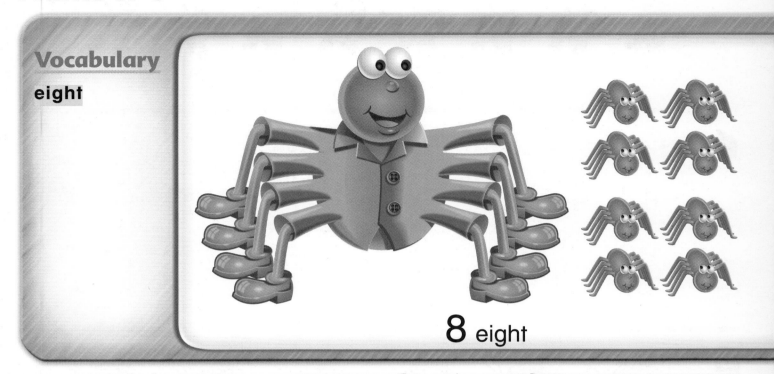

8 eight

Directions: Count the insects in each group. Use cubes to show how many insects.
Circle the groups of insects that show eight. Put an X on the groups that do not show eight.
Tell a classmate how many insects there are in each group.

Chapter 4   Lesson 2

1

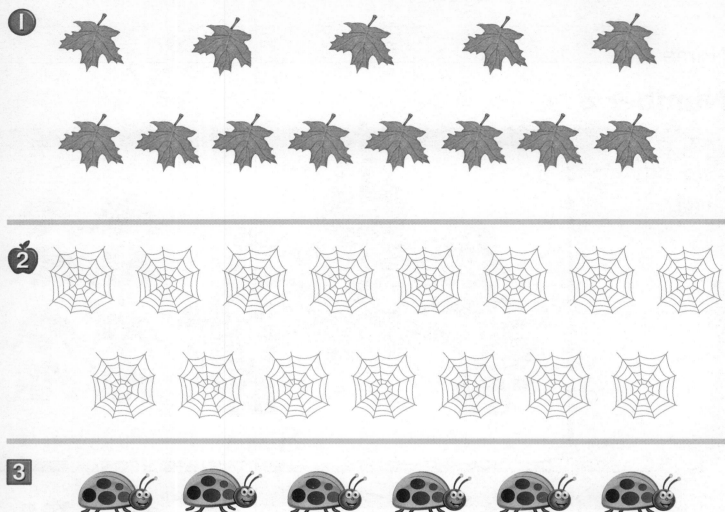

2

3

4

Directions:

1–2. Circle the group that has eight.

3–4. Count the objects. Say the number. Draw more to make a group of 8. Talk with a classmate to find out how many more you should draw.

Math at Home Activity: Draw a picture of a penny jar. Ask your child to trace 8 pennies. Have your child color and cut the pennies out and glue them on the jar. Count the pennies.

Name _____

Read and Write 6, 7, and 8

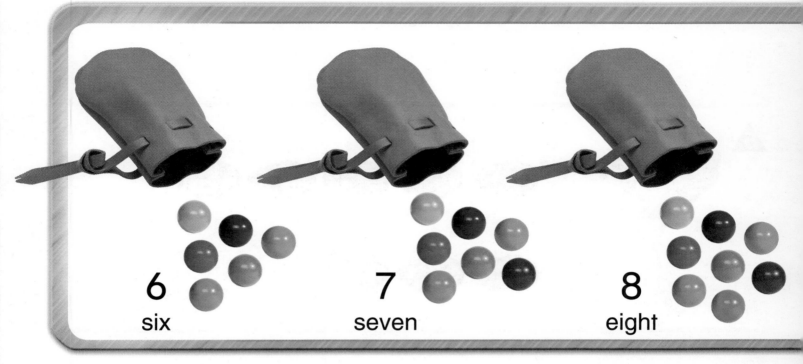

6
six

7
seven

8
eight

①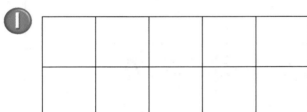

②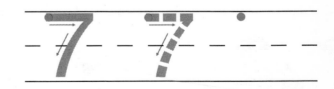

③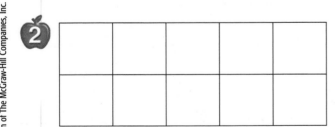

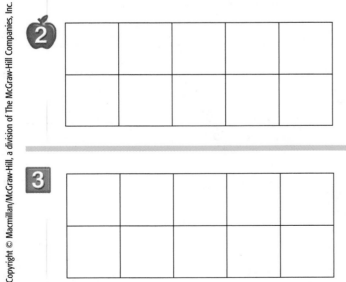

Directions:
1. Draw 6 marbles. Say the number. Trace and write the number.
2. Draw 7 marbles. Say the number. Trace and write the number.
3. Draw 8 marbles. Say the number. Trace and write the number.

Chapter 4   Lesson 3

_____

‒ ‒ ‒ ‒ ‒ ‒ ‒

_____

_____

‒ ‒ ‒ ‒ ‒ ‒ ‒

_____

_____

‒ ‒ ‒ ‒ ‒ ‒ ‒

_____

 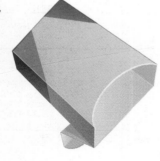

_____

‒ ‒ ‒ ‒ ‒ ‒ ‒

_____

Directions:

4‒7. Count the objects in each row. Say the number. Use WorkMat 5 and counters to show the number. Write the number.

 Math at Home Activity: Using six index cards help your child make 2 cards with 6 dots, 7 dots, and 8 dots. Write each number. Play a matching game.

Chapter 4   Lesson 3

Name _____

1

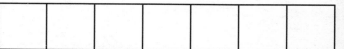

2

3

_ _ _ _ _ _ _

Directions:
1. Count the objects. Color one box for each object in that group.
2. Circle the groups of shoes that show eight. Put an X on the groups that do not show eight.
3. Count the objects. Write the number.

Game Time

Surf's Up!
Counting

You Will Need

Play with a partner. Take turns.

○ Roll 5.

○ Move your ▢ that number of squares.

○ Take a color tile each time you land on a surfboard.

○ When you reach the finish, count your color tiles.

○ The winner has the most color tiles.

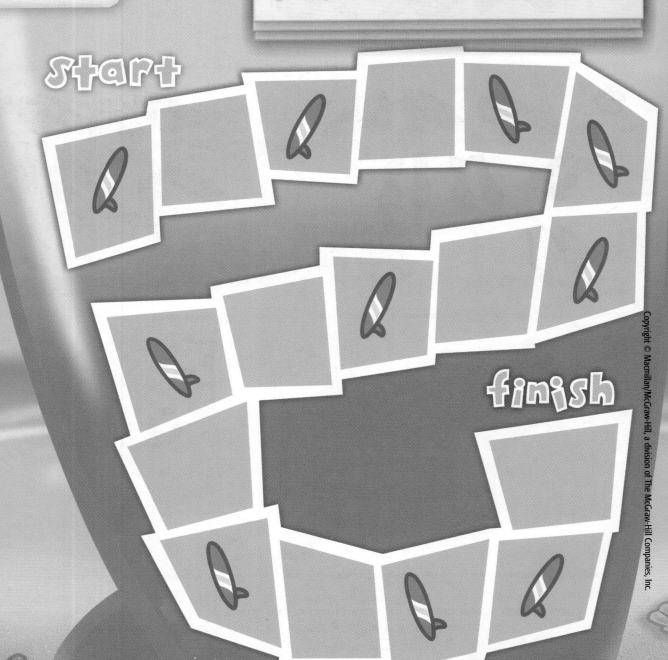

Start

finish

Name _____

Numbers 9 and 10

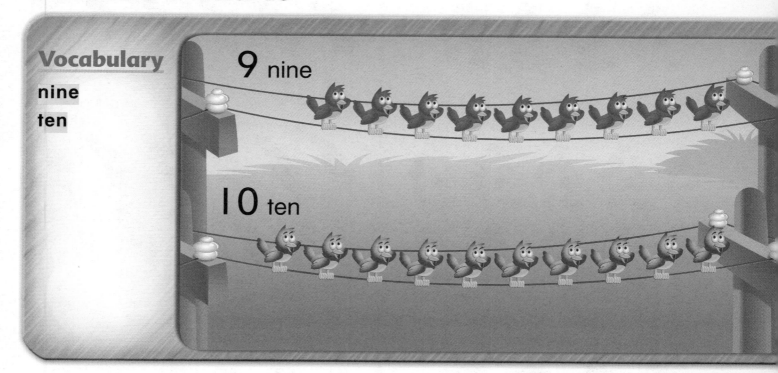

Vocabulary

nine

ten

9 nine

10 ten

①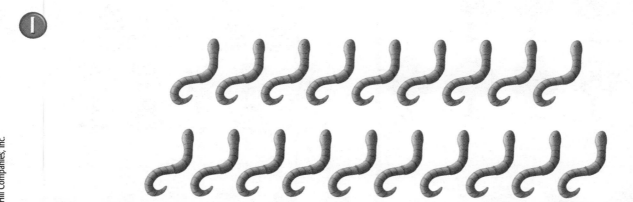

②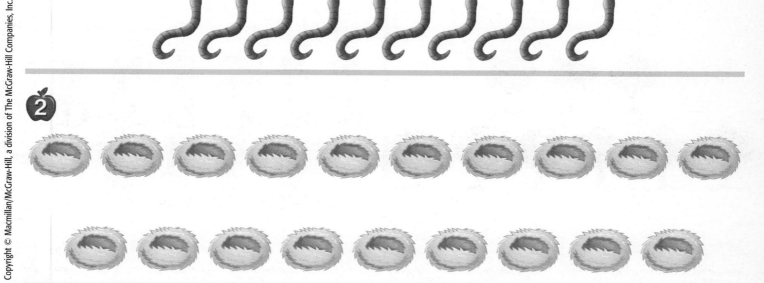

Directions:

1–2. Count the objects in each row. Say the number. Use counters to show how many objects.
Draw a red circle around the group of nine. Draw a blue circle around the group of ten.

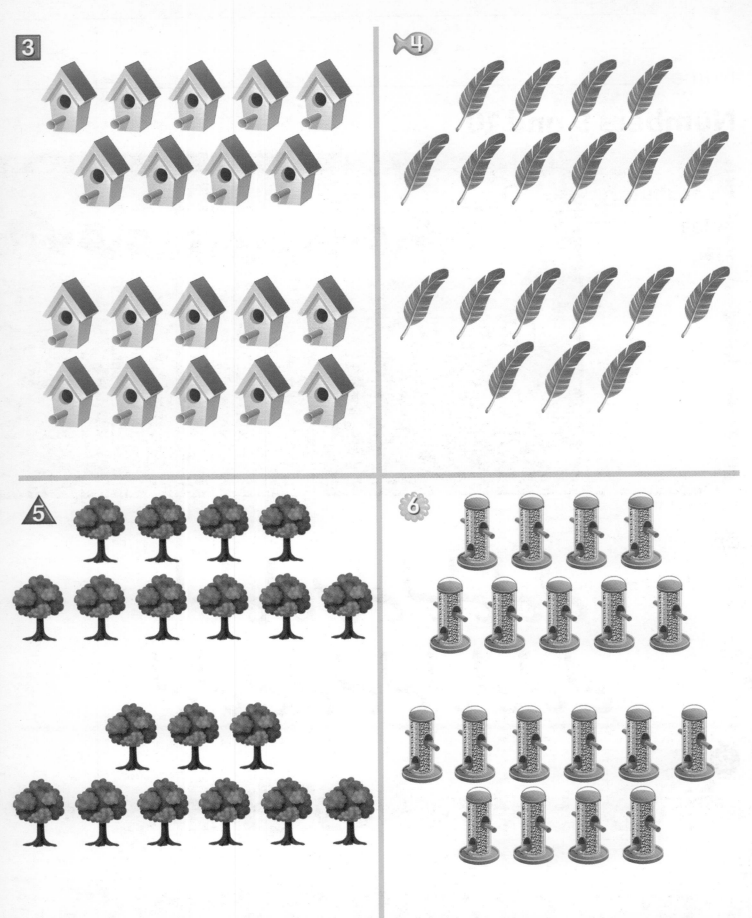

Directions:

3–6. Count the objects in each group. Say the number. Draw a red circle around the group of nine. Draw a blue circle around the group of ten.

Math at Home Activity: Use 2 colored sheets of paper. Tear each sheet into 12 pieces. Ask your child to count out 9 pieces of one color and 10 pieces of the other color.

Read and Write Numbers 9 and 10

9
nine

10
ten

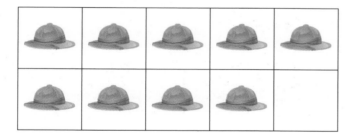

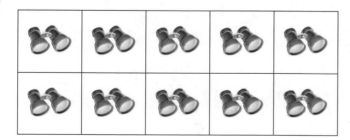

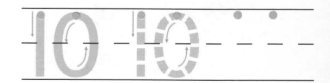

Directions:
1–2. Count the objects. Say the number. Trace and write the number.

3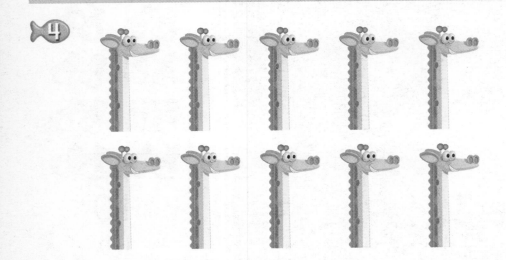

_____
_ _ _ _
_____

4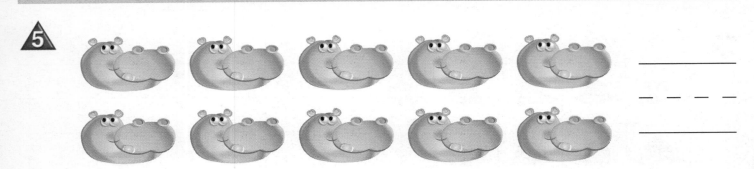

_____
_ _ _ _
_____

5

_____
_ _ _ _
_____

6

_____
_ _ _ _
_____

Directions:

3–6. Count the animals. Say the number. Use WorkMat 5 and counters to show the number. Write the number.

 Math at Home Activity: Use a book with numbered pages. Ask your child to count the pages to page nine and write nine. Then count pages to 10 and write 10.

Chapter 4   Lesson 5

Name _____

Problem-Solving Strategy

Draw a Picture

How many at the circus?

 ①

②

8

9

Directions:

1–2. Look at the picture. Find a set of objects that has the number shown. Draw those objects.

Directions:

3–6. Look at the picture. Find a set of objects that
has the number shown. Draw those objects.

Math at Home Activity: Take advantage of problem-solving
opportunities during daily routines such as riding in the car,
bedtime, doing laundry, putting away groceries, planning
schedules, and so on.

Compare Numbers to 10

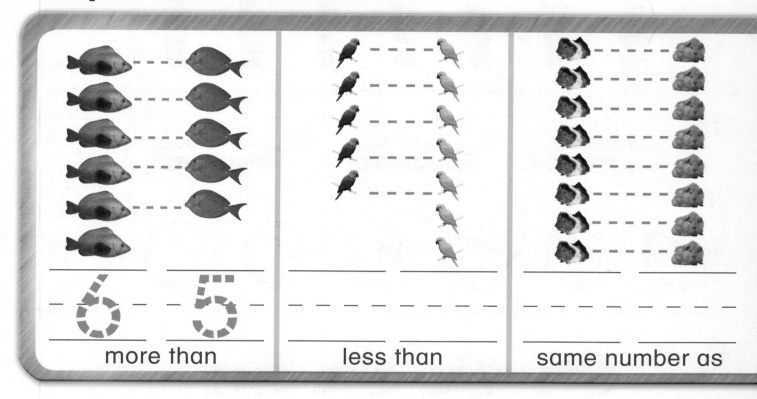

| more than | less than | same number as |

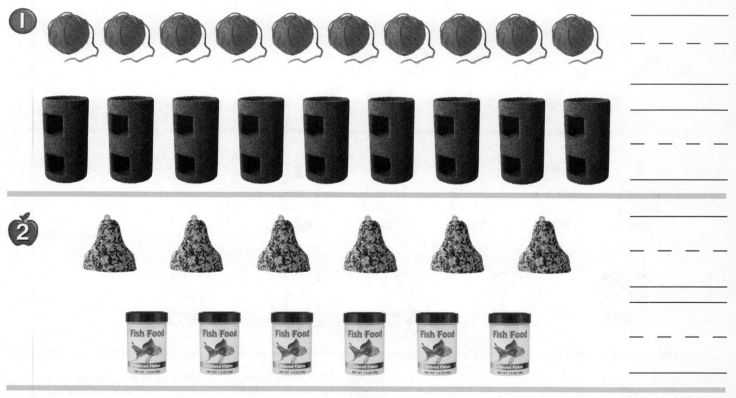

Directions:

1–2. Draw lines to match objects in one group with objects in the other. Write the numbers. Circle the number and group that has more. Put an X on the number and group that has less. Put a box around the number groups if there are the same number in each group.

3

_____

_____

_____

_____

4

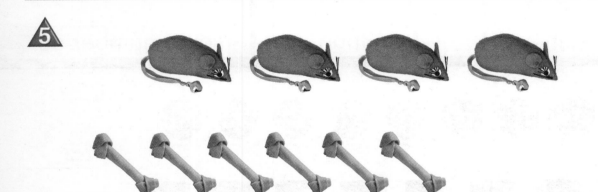

_____

_____

_____

_____

5

_____

_____

_____

_____

6

_____

_____

_____

_____

Directions:

3–6. Draw lines to match objects in one group with objects in the other. Write the numbers. Circle the number and group that are more. Put an X on the number and group that are less. Put a box around the groups if there are the same number in each group.

Math at Home Activity: Make two different groups of 10 items or less. Ask your child which group has more, less, or if they have the same number of items. Write the number.

Chapter 4   Lesson 7

Order Numbers to 10

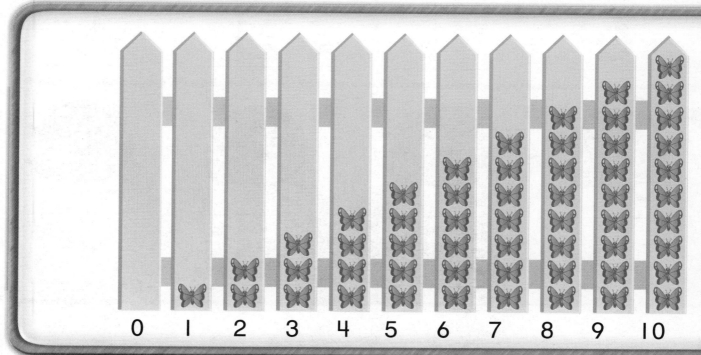

0 1 2 3 4 5 6 7 8 9 10

1

0   1   2   3   ____

2

6   7   8   ____   10

Directions:
1–2. Count the objects. Trace the numbers. Write the missing number that comes
just before or just after.

Chapter 4   Lesson 8

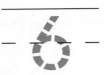 _____ **6** _____   _____ _____   _____ **8** _____   _____ **9** _____

 **3**   **4**   **5**   _____ _____

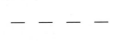 _____ _____   **6**   _____ _____   **8**

 2   _____ _____   _____ _____   _____ _____

Directions:

3–4. Count the seeds and circles on the objects. Trace the numbers. Write the missing number that comes before or after.

5–6. Count the boxes and petals on the objects. Write the missing numbers that come before and after. Draw the missing items on the object.

 Math at Home Activity: Cut small squares. Ask your child to number them one to 10. Shuffle. Ask your child to order them. Count again.

118   one hundred eighteen

Chapter 4   Lesson 8

Name _____

Ordinal Numbers

Vocabulary

ordinal numbers

first   second   third   fourth   fifth

Directions:
1. Draw a circle around the first armadillo. Put an X on the fourth armadillo.
2. Draw a circle around the second jackrabbit. Put an X on the fifth jackrabbit.

Directions: Name the position of each vulture. Circle the sixth vulture. Put an X on the third vulture Name the position of each snake. Circle the first snake. The brown lizard is first. Name the position of each lizard. Put an X on the seventh lizard.

 Math at Home Activity: Line up a row of ten stuffed animals or toys all facing the same direction. Have your child tell you which animal is first, sixth, tenth, and fourth.

Nests are in a tree.

Winter

How many nests do you see?

I see _____ nests.

Spring

Problem Solving
in Science

Real-World MATH

There are lots of things on trees.
Take a look.

This book belongs to

_____

Birds are in the tree.

Autumn

How many birds do you see?

I see _____ birds.

Apples are on the tree.

Summer

How many apples do you see?

I see _____ apples.

Name _____

A. 8

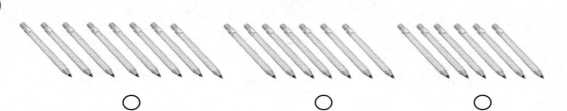

           ○   ○   ○

B.

     ○   ○   ○

1.

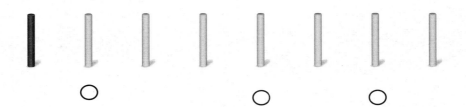

     ○   ○   ○

2. 10

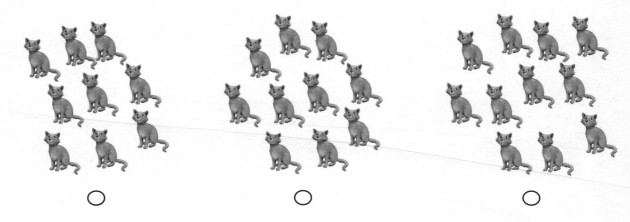

     ○   ○   ○

Directions: Listen as your teacher reads the problem.
Choose the best answer.

3.

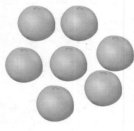

◯　　　　　　◯　　　　　　◯

4.

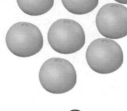  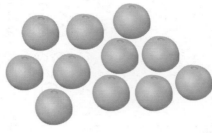

◯　　　　　　◯　　　　　　◯

5.

◯　　　　　　◯　　　　　　◯

6. 9

◯　　　　　　◯　　　　　　◯

Directions: Listen as your teacher reads the problem.
Choose the best answer.

Summative Assessment

Construct and Use Graphs

> ▶ **Key Vocabulary**
> data
> real graph
> picture graph

Explore

What is this picture showing?

Are there more red handprints or blue handprints?

Name _____

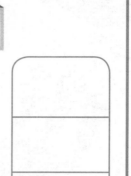

① ② ③

_____   _____

_ _ _ _ _ _ _ _   _ _ _ _ _ _ _ _

_____   _____

Directions:
1. Color one box for each doll to show how many dolls.
2. Color one box for each block to show how many blocks.
3. Color one box for each ball to show how many balls.
4. Count the bears in each group. Write the number. Circle the group that shows more.

This page checks skills needed for Chapter 5.

MATH at HOME

Dear Family,

Today my class started Chapter 5, **Construct and Use Graphs**. I will be learning to make and read graphs. Here are my vocabulary words, an activity we can do, and a list of books we can read together.

Love, _____

Activity

Have your child ask family members if their favorite juice is orange, grape, or apple. Record their answers on a graph. Ask your child questions about the information on the graph. Have your child ask you questions about the data on the graph.

Key Vocabulary

data

Favorite Foods	
Food	Votes
🍎	IIII
🌽	III
🥔	IIIII III

real graph graph using real objects

picture graph

Our Favorite Pets							
Cats	🐱	🐱					
Dogs	🐕	🐕	🐕	🐕			
Fish	🐟						

Math Online Click on the eGlossary link at tx.grKmath.com to find out more about these words. There are 13 languages.

Books to Read

Tiger Math: Learning to Graph from a Baby Tiger
by Ann Whitehead Nagda
Henry Holt & Company, 2002.

The Best Vacation Ever
by Stuart J. Murphy
Harper Trophy, 1997.

Anno's Flea Market
by Mitsumasa Anno
Penguin Group Incorporated, 1984.

MATEMÁTICAS en CASA

Estimada familia:

Hoy mi clase comenzó el Capítulo 5, **Construye y usa gráficas**. Aprenderé a hacer y a leer gráficas. A continuación, están mis palabras de vocabulario, una actividad que podemos realizar y una lista de libros que podemos leer juntos.

Cariños, _____

Actividad

Inventen sondeos para su familia. Por ejemplo, pídanle a su hijo(a) que les pregunte a sus parientes si su jugo favorito es el jugo de naranjas, uvas o manzanas. Anoten sus respuestas en una gráfica. Háganle preguntas a su hijo(a) acerca de la información en la gráfica. Pídanle a su hijo(a) que les haga preguntas acerca de los datos en la gráfica.

Vocabulario clave

Datos

Favorite Foods	
Food	Votes
🍎	卌
🍌	|||
🌭	卌 |||

Gráfica real Una gráfica que usa objetos reales.

Pictograma

Nuestros animales domésticos favorito	
Gatos	🐱🐱
Perros	🐶🐶🐶🐶
Pescados	🐟

Math Online Visiten el enlace eGlossary en tx.grKmath.com para averiguar más sobre estas palabras, las cuales se muestran en 13 idiomas.

Libros recomendados

¿Hagamos una grafia?
de Lisa Trumbauer
Yellow Umbrella Books, 2005.

Más máthematicas con los chocolates de m&m's
de Barbara Barbieri McGrath
Charlesbridge Publishing, 2001.

Collect and Record Data

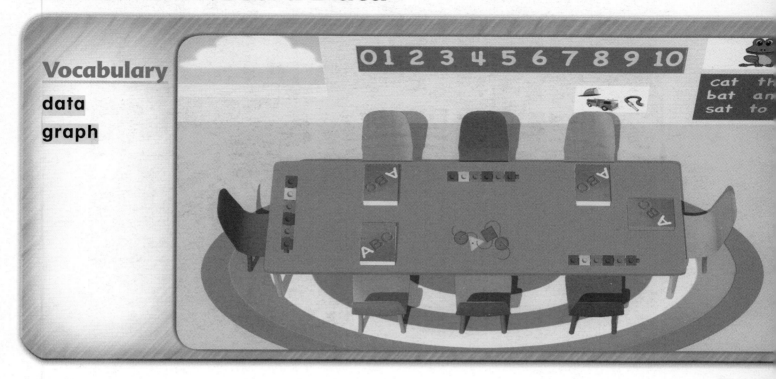

Vocabulary

data

graph

 _____

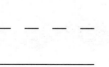 _____

 _____

Directions:

1. Place a yellow color tile on the graph for each cube train. Place a red color tile on the graph for each book. Place a green color tile on the graph for each necklace. Color the boxes to match. Write the number.

Chapter 5   Lesson 1   one hundred thirty-one   131

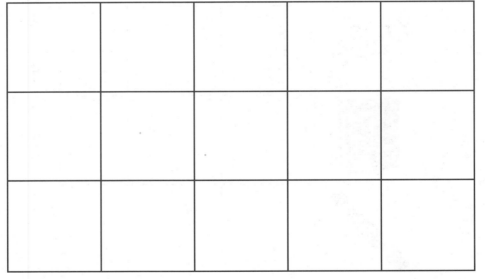

Directions:

2. Place a green color tile on the graph for each car.
   Place a yellow color tile on the graph for each bus.
   Place a red color tile on the graph for each bike.
   Color the boxes to match. Write the number.

Math at Home Activity: Draw a picture of some of the items in a kitchen cupboard. Color boxes to show how many of each item. Write the number of each.

Chapter 5 Lesson 1

Real Graphs

Vocabulary
real graph

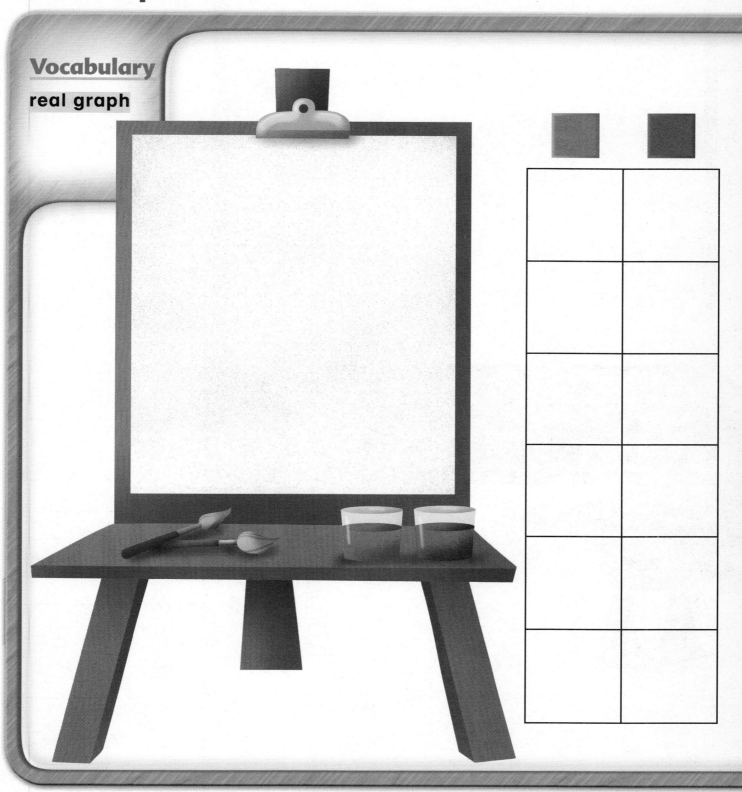

Directions: Use red and blue color tiles to make a picture. Sort your tiles by color on the graph. Which group has more tiles? Circle it.

Chapter 5   Lesson 2

Directions: Use yellow and green color tiles to make a picture on the chalkboard. Sort your tiles by color. Put them on the graph. Tell about the graph. Which group has less tiles? Circle it.

Math at Home Activity: Toss 9 pennies. Sort heads and tails. Graph results as done above. Tell which has more and less.

Problem-Solving Strategy
Look For a Pattern

What do you see?

Directions: Write the number of checkers in each column on the lines below the graph. Discuss the pattern of numbers and colors.

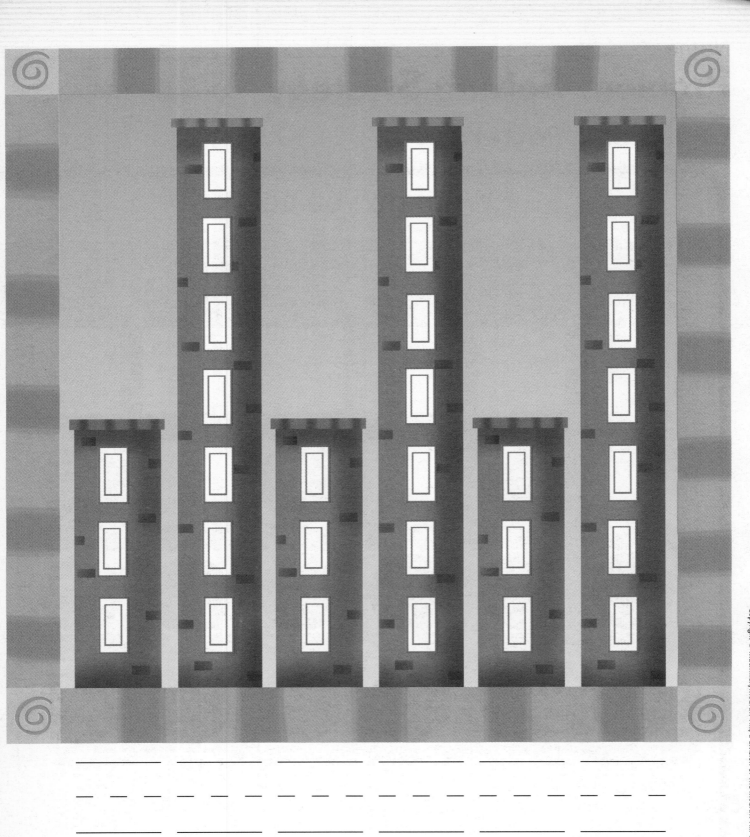

_____ _____ _____

— — — — — — — — — — — —

_____ _____ _____

Directions: Create an AB pattern by coloring a different number of windows in each building. Have a partner write the numbers that show how many windows you colored in each building. Discuss the pattern of numbers and colors.

Math at Home Activity: Take advantage of problem-solving opportunities during daily routines such as riding in the car, bedtime, doing laundry, putting away groceries, planning schedules, and so on.

Name

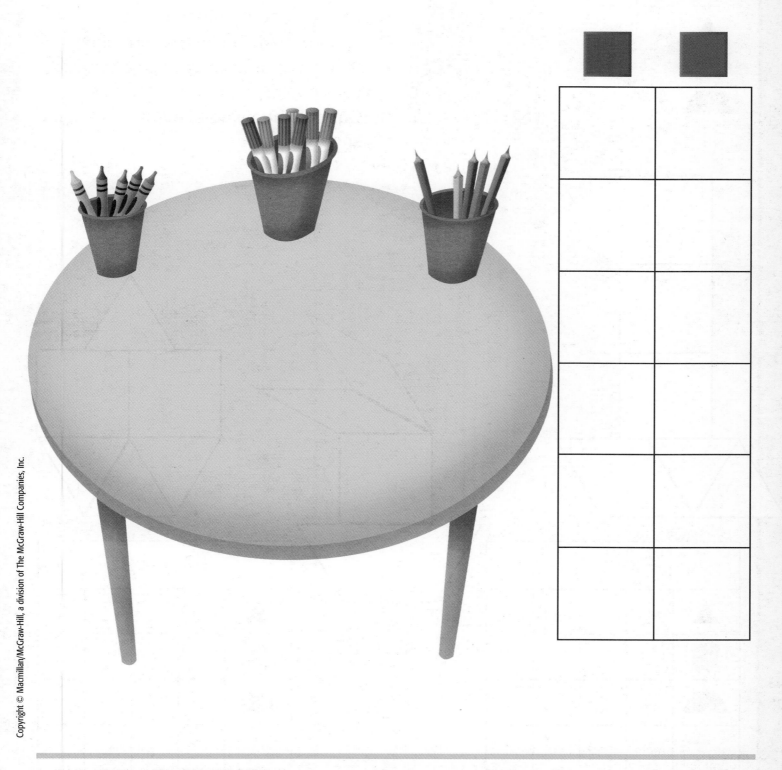

Directions: Use color tiles to make a picture on the table. Sort your tiles by color.
Put them on the graph. Which group has more tiles? Circle it.

Boat Building
Graphing

Play with a partner:
- ⦾ 2 players.
- ⦾ Choose one boat each.
- ⦾ Build the boat using pattern blocks.
- ⦾ Graph the shapes you used to build your boat by coloring the boxes.
- ⦾ Count to see who used more of each shape.

You Will Need

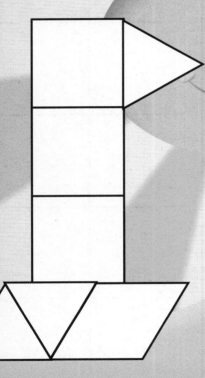

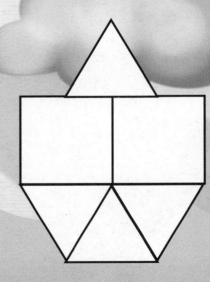

Player 1				
▲				
■				
▬				
╱				
◢				

Player 2				
▲				
■				
▬				
╱				
◢				

Picture Graphs

Vocabulary

picture graph

Which pet do you like more?

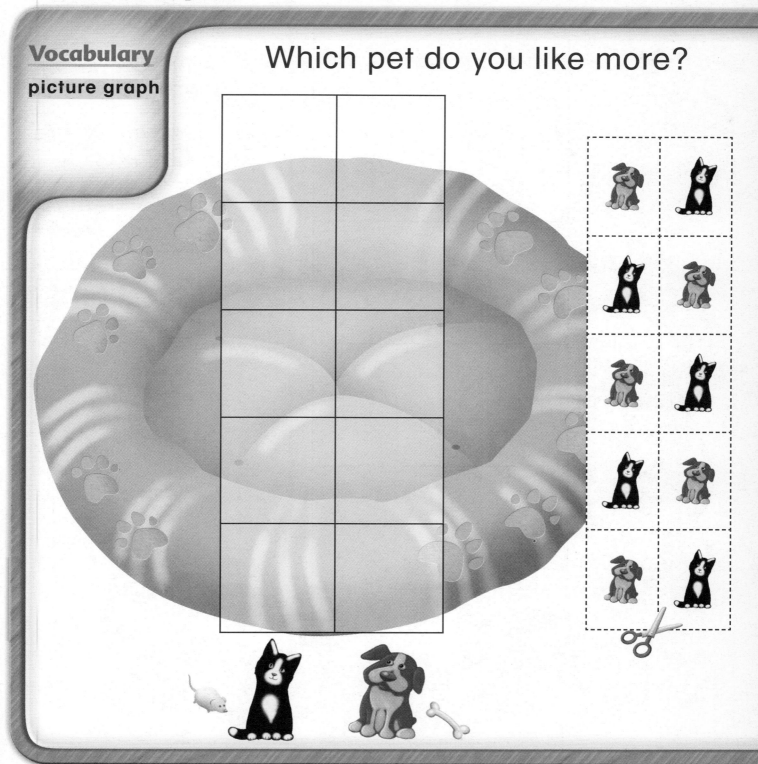

Directions: Ask five students which pet they would rather have. Cut and glue the picture of the pet on the graph. Which group has more pets? Circle it. Talk with a classmate about your graph.

Which place would you like to play?

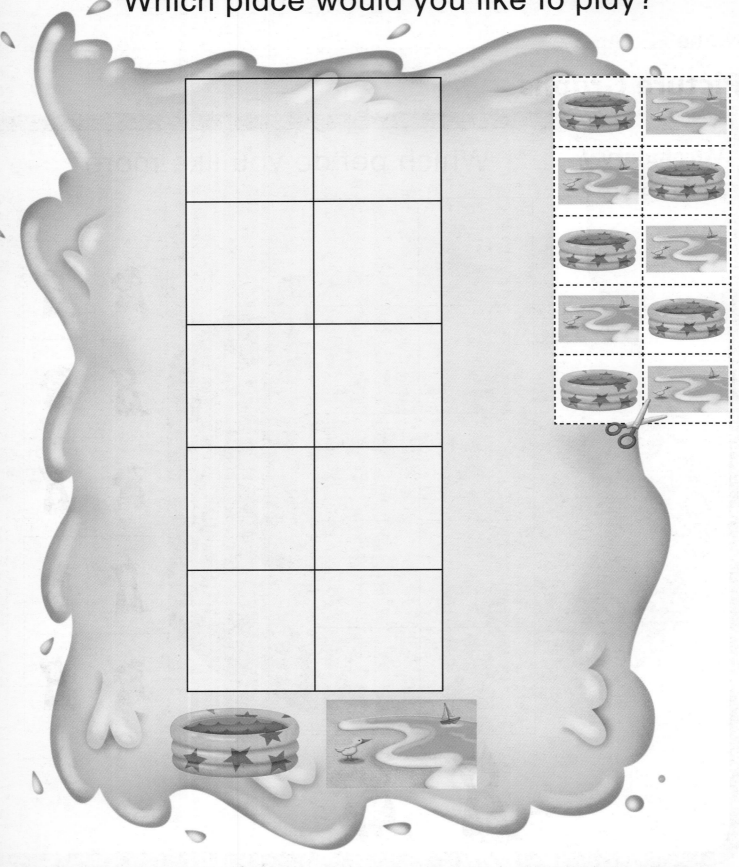

Directions: Ask five students if they would rather play at the beach or in a pool. Cut and glue the picture each student chose on the graph. Which group has less places? Circle it. Talk with a classmate about your graph.

Math at Home Activity: Gather toys such as dominos, cars, and figurines. Sort the toys in two groups. Make a picture graph of each toy. Circle the group that shows more.

Name _____

Make a Graph

Vocabulary

survey

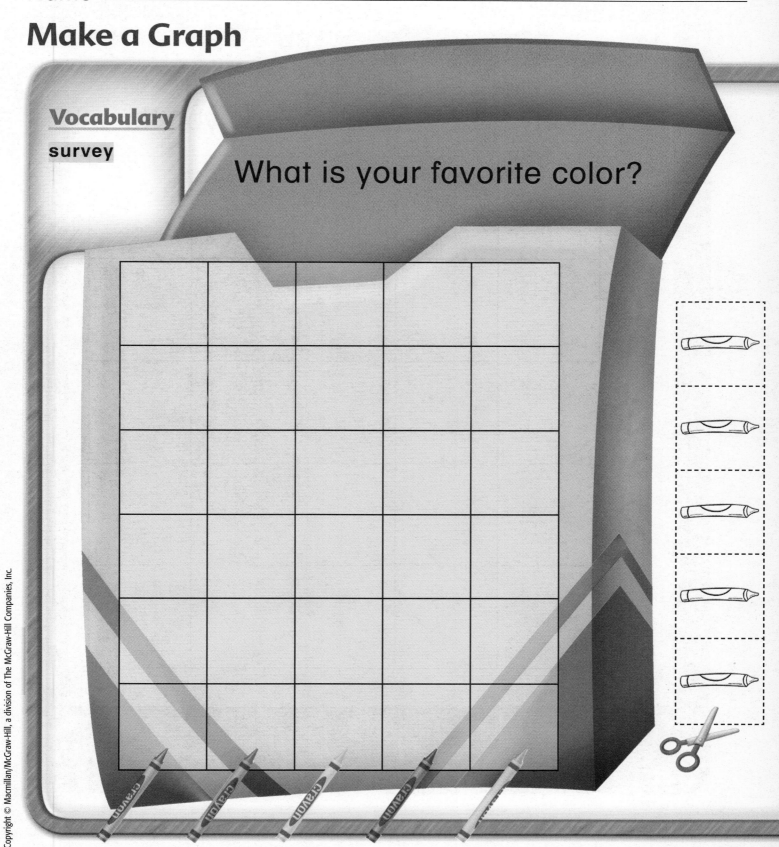

What is your favorite color?

Directions: Ask five students this question: which of these colors: red, green, yellow, blue, or orange is your favorite color? Use that color crayon to color one of the crayons in the dashed boxes. Cut and paste the dashed boxes on the graph. Talk with a classmate about your graph.

How many _____ do you have?

5					
4					
3					
2					
1					

Directions: Decide on a question. Fill in the blank. Ask five students to answer the question. Fill in the graph to show their answers.

Math at Home Activity: Cut red and blue circles from paper. Ask family members which color is their favorite. Make a picture graph with the circles. Which color do people like the most?

Chapter 5   Lesson 5

What is your favorite 4th of July activity? Ask 5 students.

Problem Solving in Social Studies

Real-World MATH

We celebrate on the 4th of July. Some people march in parades.

This book belongs to

_____

Here is a graph. It shows what Juan's friends like to do on the 4th of July.

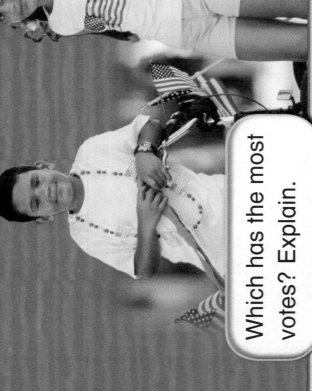

Which has the most votes? Explain.

Some people have picnics.

Name _____

A.

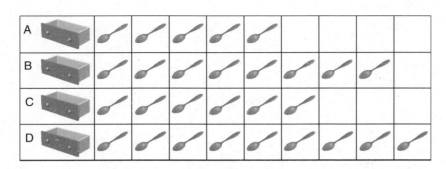

8   6   5

◯   ◯   ◯

B.

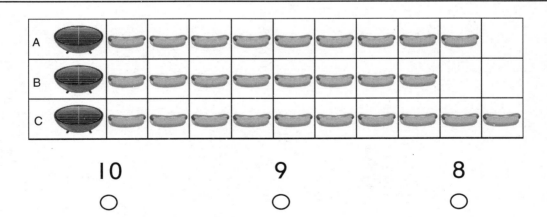

◯   ◯   ◯

1.

10   9   8

◯   ◯   ◯

Directions: Listen as your teacher reads the problem. Choose the best answer.

2.

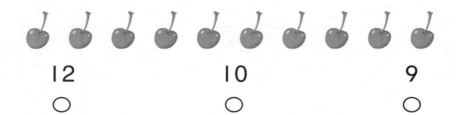

○   ○   ○

3.

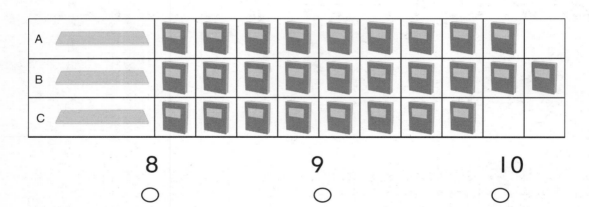

12	10	9
○	○	○

4.

A										
B										
C										

8	9	10
○	○	○

5.

○   ○   ○

Directions: Listen as your teacher reads the problem. Choose the best answer.

Summative Assessment

CHAPTER

6

Use Numbers to 20

Key Vocabulary

twenty

Explore

Draw a circle on the people puppets and a box on the animal puppets.

Are there more people puppets or animal puppets?

Name _____

 ①

_____

- - - - - - - -

_____

 ②

_____

- - - - - - - -

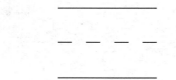

_____

- - - - - - - -

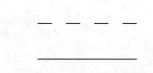

_____

- - - - - - - -

③

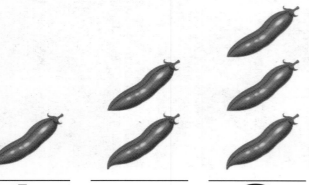

| **1** | | **3** |

 ④

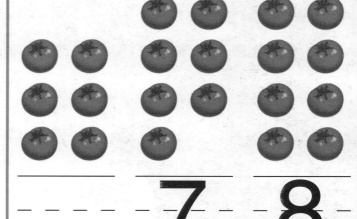

| **7** | **8** |

Directions:

1. Count the carrots. Write the number.

2. Count the ears of corn in each group. Write the number.

3–4. Write the missing numbers.

150   one hundred fifty

This page checks skills needed for Chapter 6.

Dear Family,

Today my class started Chapter 6, **Use Numbers to 20**. I will be learning to count and order numbers to 20. Here is my vocabulary word, an activity we can do, and a list of books we can read together.

Love, _____

Activity

Have your child find 20 or less of an object. For example, have your child find 13 pennies or 17 crayons. Count the objects. Write the number. Compare to show more, less, or equal amounts.

Key Vocabulary

twenty

20

2 tens

Math Online Click on the eGlossary link at tx.grKmath.com to find out more about these words. There are 13 languages.

Books to Read

Gathering : A Northwoods Counting Book
by Betsy Bowen
Houghton Mifflin
Company, 1999.

Let's Count It Out, Jesse Bear
by Nancy White Carlstrom
Aladdin, 2001.

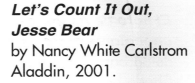

How Many Snails?
by Paul Giganti
HarperCollins
Publishers, 1994.

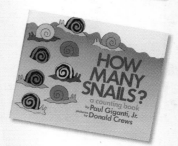

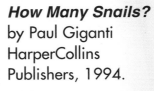

MATEMÁTICAS en CASA

Estimada familia:

Hoy mi clase comenzó el Capítulo 6, **Usa los números hasta el 20**. Aprenderé a contar y a ordenar los números hasta el 20. A continuación, está mi palabra de vocabulario, una actividad que podemos realizar y una lista de libros que podemos leer juntos.

Cariños,

_____

Actividad

Hagan que su hijo(a) busque 20 ó menos de un objeto. Por ejemplo, pídanle que busque 13 monedas de 1¢ ó 17 crayones. Cuenten los objetos. Escriban el número. Comparen para mostrar más, menos o cantidades iguales.

Vocabulario clave

veinte

20

2 decenas

 **Math Online** Visiten el enlace eGlossary en tx.grKmath.com para averiguar más sobre estas palabras, las cuales se muestran en 13 idiomas.

Libros para leer

El libro de contar de los chocolates marca m&m
de Barbara Barbieri McGrath
Charlesbridge
Publishing, 1996.

Cuenta con el beisbol
de Barbara Barbieri McGrath
Charlesbridge Publishing, 2005.

Name _____

Numbers 11 and 12

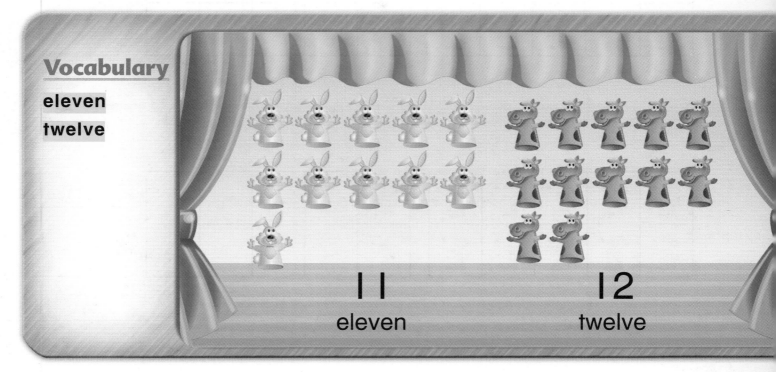

11
eleven

12
twelve

  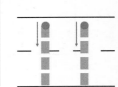

  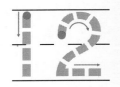

Directions:
1–2. Count the objects. Say the number. Use WorkMat 6 and
counters to show the number. Trace and write the number.

Chapter 6   Lesson 1

one hundred fifty-three   153

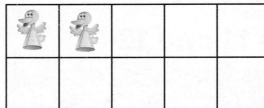

4

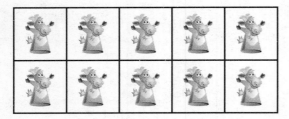

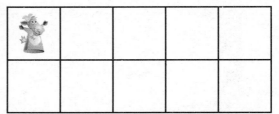

5

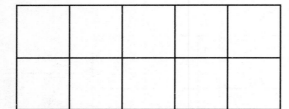

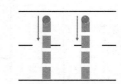

6

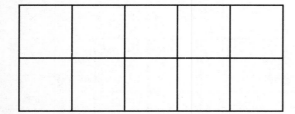

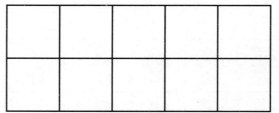

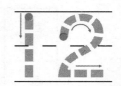

Directions:

3–4. Count the objects. Say the number. Use WorkMat 6 and counters to show the numbers. Write the number.

5–6. Say the number. Trace the number. Use counters to count the number. Draw circles for counters to show the number.

 Math at Home Activity: Use an empty egg carton. Ask your child to fill each egg holder with one item. Use the items to count 11 and 12. Write each number.

Chapter 6   Lesson 1

Numbers 16 and 17

Vocabulary

sixteen

seventeen

16
sixteen

17
seventeen

1

 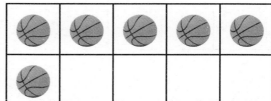 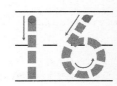

2

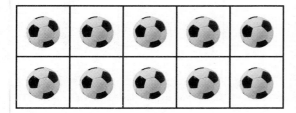 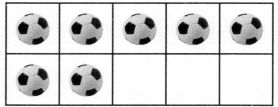 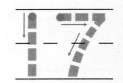

Directions:

1–2. Count the objects. Say the number. Use WorkMat 6
and counters to show the number. Trace the number.

Chapter 6   Lesson 3

one hundred fifty-seven   **157**

3

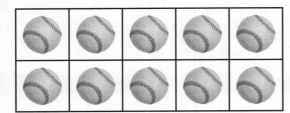 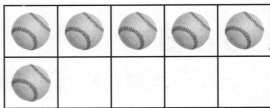

_____

- - - - - - - - - -

_____

4

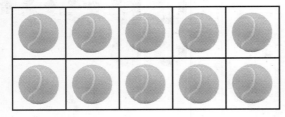 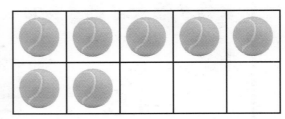

_____

- - - - - - - - - -

_____

5

 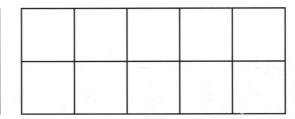

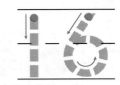

6

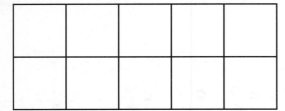 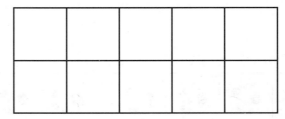

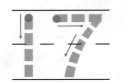

Directions:

3–4. Count the objects. Say the number.
Use WorkMat 6 and counters to show
the number. Write the number.

5–6. Say the number. Trace the number. Use
WorkMat 6 and counters to count the number.
Draw circles for counters to show the number.

 Math at Home Activity: Ask your child to make groups of
16 and 17 using dry macaroni. Have your child show how each
group has 10 and 6 or 7 more and then write 16 and 17.

158   one hundred fifty-eight

Chapter 6   Lesson 3

Name _____

 1

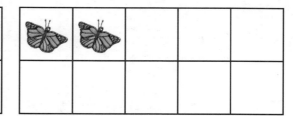

_____

- - - - - - - - -

 2

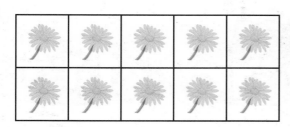

_____

- - - - - - - - -

_____

3

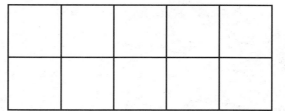

4

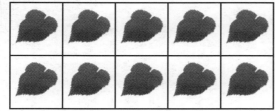

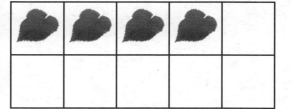

Directions:
1–2. Count the objects. Write the number.
3. Draw more cherries to make 14.
4. Draw more leaves to make 17.

Leap Frog!

Recognizing Numbers to 17

Play with a partner. Take turns.
- Roll the [5].
- Move your cube that many spaces.
- If you land on another player's cube, or on a frog, you may "leap" over it to the next space.
- The first player to 17 wins.

START

FINISH

Name _____

Problem-Solving Strategy
Look for a Pattern

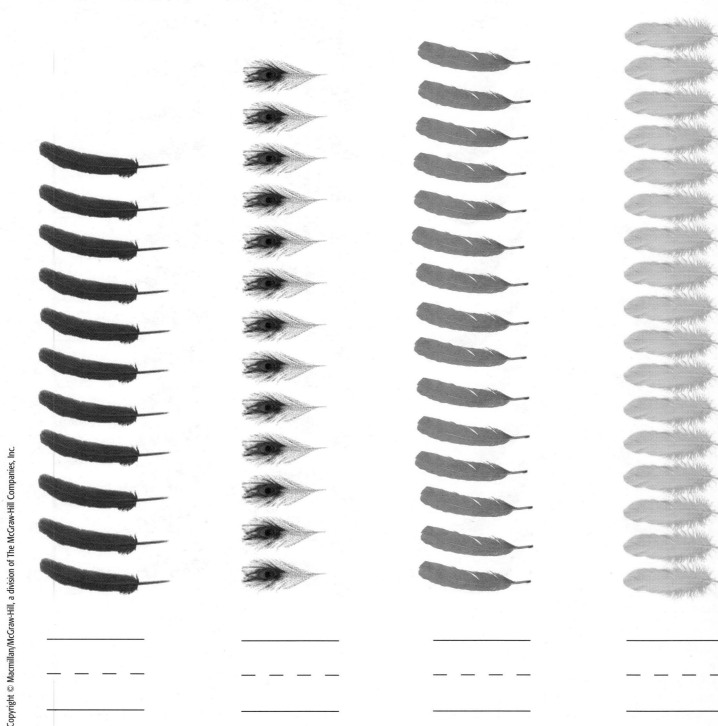

_____   _____   _____   _____

- - - - - - - -   - - - - - - - -   - - - - - - - -   - - - - - - - -

_____   _____   _____   _____

Directions:
Count the feathers. Write the number. What pattern do you notice in the numbers?

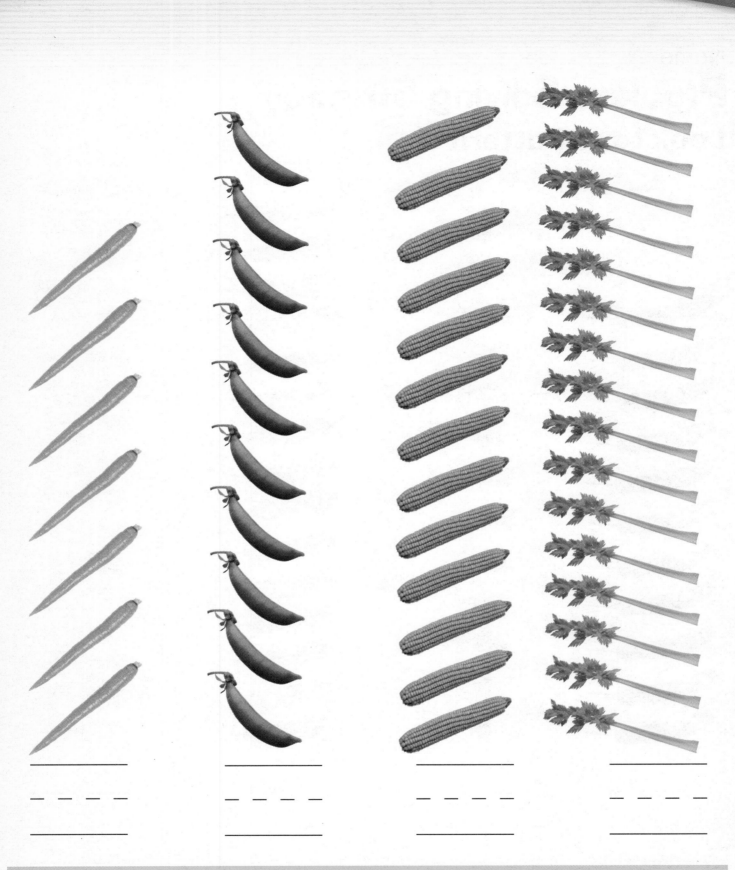

_____

- - - - - - - -

_____

Directions:
Count the vegetables. Write the number.
What pattern do you notice in the numbers?

 Math at Home Activity: Take advantage of problem-solving opportunities during daily routines. When on a walk help your child count and record the number of cars and trucks he or she sees. Discuss how this data could be displayed.

Name _____

Numbers 18, 19, and 20

Vocabulary

eighteen

nineteen

twenty

18	19	20
eighteen	nineteen	twenty

①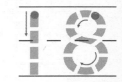

②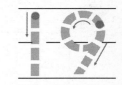

③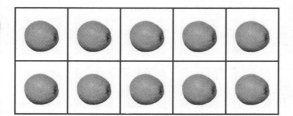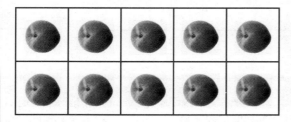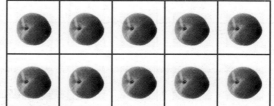

Directions:

1–3. Count the objects by counting on from 10. Say the number.
Use WorkMat 6 and counters to show the number. Trace the number.

Chapter 6   Lesson 5   one hundred sixty-three   **163**

4

 _____
- - - - - - -
_____

 5

 _____
- - - - - - -
_____

6

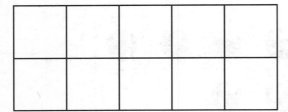 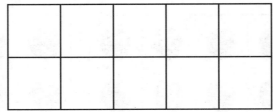 

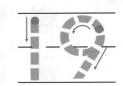

7

 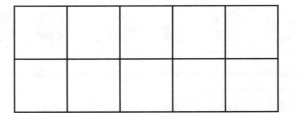

Directions:

4–5. Count the objects. Say the number. Use WorkMat 6 and counters to show the numbers. Write the number.

6–7. Say the number. Trace the number. Use WorkMat 6 and counters to count the number. Draw circles for counters to show the number.

Math at Home Activity: Draw a piggy bank on paper. Count coins in groups of 18, 19, and 20. Place a group of coins on the piggy bank. Write the number. Repeat for other numbers.

Chapter 6   Lesson 5

Compare Numbers to 20

_____   _____   _____   _____

is more than   same number

1

_____   _____

2

_____   _____

Directions:
1–2. Count the objects. Write the number. Draw an X through
the number that describes the group with more objects.

3

 **4**

_____

_ _ _ _ _

_____

_____

_ _ _ _ _

_____

5

6

_____

_ _ _ _ _

_____

8   10

Directions:

3–5. Count the objects. Write the number. Circle
the number that shows less. Put a box
around the numbers that are equal.

6. Draw circles on each plate to show the
number. Circle the number that shows less.

 Math at Home Activity: Make groups of buttons with
various amounts to 20. Ask your child to count the buttons and
tell which group has more, less, or is equal.

166 one hundred sixty-six

Chapter 6 Lesson 6

Name _____

Order Numbers to 20

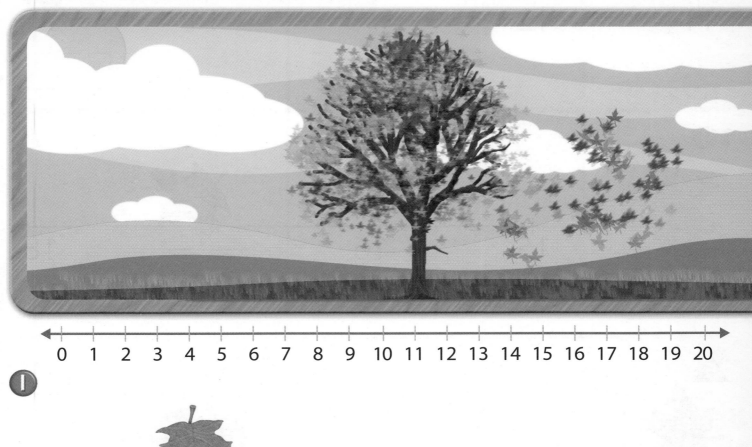

0 1 2 3 4 5 6 7 8 9 10 11 12 13 14 15 16 17 18 19 20

1

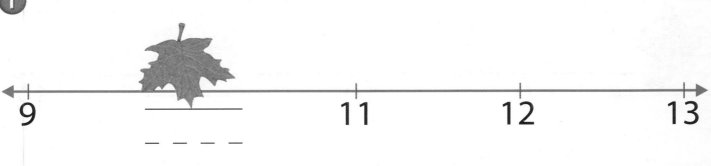

9 ____ 11 12 13

2

____ 16 17 ____ 19

Directions:
1–2. Write the missing number(s).

3

11   12   ＿＿＿   14   ＿＿＿

4

＿＿＿   15   16   ＿＿＿   18

5

＿＿＿   9   10   ＿＿＿   12

6

16   ＿＿＿   18   19   ＿＿＿

Directions:
3–6. Write the missing numbers.

Math at Home Activity: Cut squares and number them from 0 to 20. Show any five numbers in number order. Hide one number. Ask your child which number is missing.

There are postcard collections.

GRAND CANYON

Statue of Liberty, NY

SEATTLE SPACE NEEDLE

Yellowstone National Park

Welcome to the Alamo

Bridge

How many postcards are here?

_____ postcards

.D DOWN

Problem Solving
in Social Studies

Real-World MATH

Some people have collections.
A collection is many of the same
kind of thing.

This book belongs to

_____

There are coin collections.

How many coins are here?

___ coins

There are stamp collections.

How many stamps are here?

___ stamps

Name _____

1

 _____

2

 _____

3  _____

4  _____

 _____

5

16 _____ _____ 19 _____

Directions:

1–3. Count the objects. Write the number.
4. Count the objects in each group. Write the number.
   Circle the group that has more.
5. Write the hidden numbers.

Chapter 6

Name _____

1

 2

- - - - - - -

- - - - - - -

3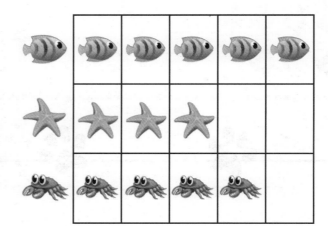

- - - - - - -

- - - - - - -

- - - - - - -

Directions:
1. Circle the object that comes next in the pattern.
2. Draw lines to match objects in one group with objects in the other.
   Write the number. Circle the number and group that are more.
3. Count the fish, star fish, and crabs. Write the number.

Name _____

A.

18	16	19
○	○	○

B.

○	○	○

1.

○	○	○

2.

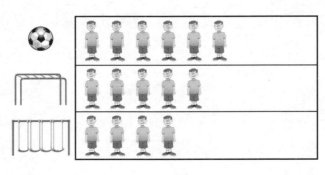

4	5	6
○	○	○

Directions: Listen as the teacher reads the problem. Choose the best answer.

3.

○   ○   ○

4.

19   18   16

○   ○   ○

---

5.   14

○   ○   ○

6.

○   ○   ○

Directions: Listen as the teacher reads the problem. Choose the best answer.

174   one hundred seventy-four

Summative Assessment

STOP

Compare Measurements

Key Vocabulary

length
weight
capacity
area
temperature

Copyright © Macmillan/McGraw-Hill, a division of The McGraw-Hill Companies, Inc.

Explore

Draw an X on the elephant that is bigger.
Draw a circle around the elephant with the shorter trunk.

Name _____

①

②

③

④

Directions:
1. Circle the pencil that is longer.
2. Circle the quilt that covers more of the bed.
3. Circle the one that can carry more people.
4. Circle the animal you could hold in your hand.

This page checks skills needed for Chapter 7.

Dear Family,

Today my class started Chapter 7, **Compare Measurements**. I will be learning about length, weight, capacity, area, and temperature. Here are my vocabulary words, an activity we can do, and a list of books we can read together.

Love,

_____

Activity

Help your child find objects that differ in length such as pencils, crayons, shoe laces, and silverware. Have your child choose 2 objects and decide which one is longer. Find objects of differing weight. Have your child choose 2 objects and decide which one is lighter.

Key Vocabulary

length

holds more the pitcher holds more than the glass

holds less the glass holds less than the pitcher

 **Math Online** Click on the eGlossary link at tx.grKmath.com to find out more about these words. There are 13 languages.

Books to Read

The Best Bug Parade
by Stuart J. Murphy
HarperCollins Publishers,
1996.

Super Sand Castle Saturday
by Stuart J. Murphy
HarperCollins Publishers,
1999.

Length
by Henry Pluckrose
Scholastic Library
Publishing, 1995.

MATEMÁTICAS en CASA

Estimada familia:

Hoy mi clase comenzó el Capítulo 7, **Compara medidas**. Aprenderé sobre la longitud, el peso, la capacidad, area, y temperature. A continuación, están mis palabras de vocabulario, una actividad que podemos realizar y una lista de libros que podemos leer juntos.

Cariños, _____

Actividad

Ayuden a su hijo(a) a encontrar objetos que difieran en longitud, como lápices, lápices de colores, cordones de zapatos y cubiertos. Pídanle a su hijo(a) que seleccione 2 objetos y decida cuál es el más largo. Busquen objetos de diferentes pesos. Pídanle a su hijo(a) que seleccione 2 objetos y que decida cuál es el más liviano.

Vocabulario clave

longitud

contiene más

contiene menos

Math Online Visiten el enlace eGlossary en tx.grKmath.com para averiguar más sobre estas palabras, las cuales se muestran en 13 idiomas.

Libros recomendados

Medir: la casita perfecta
de John Burstein
Gareth Stevens Publishing, 2006.

¿Por qué medimos?
de Lisa Trumbauer
Red Brick, 2006.

Compare Length

Vocabulary

length
longer
shorter
same as

Directions:

1. Use cubes to make a train shorter than the fish. Draw the train above the fish.
   Use cubes to make a train longer than the fish. Draw the train below the fish.

2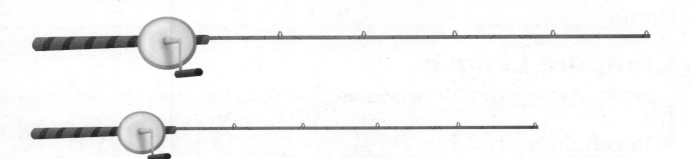

3

4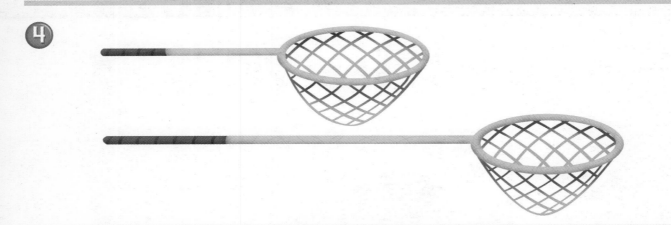

5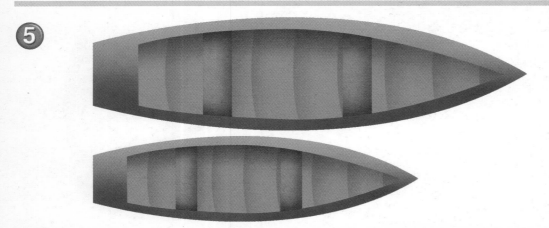

Directions:

2–5. For each set of pictures, put an X on the object that is shorter. Circle the object that is longer. If the objects are the same length underline them.

Math at Home Activity: Place a spoon and pencil, or straw and crayon on a table, one above the other. Have your child tell which is longer and which is shorter.

Order Length

Vocabulary

shortest

longest

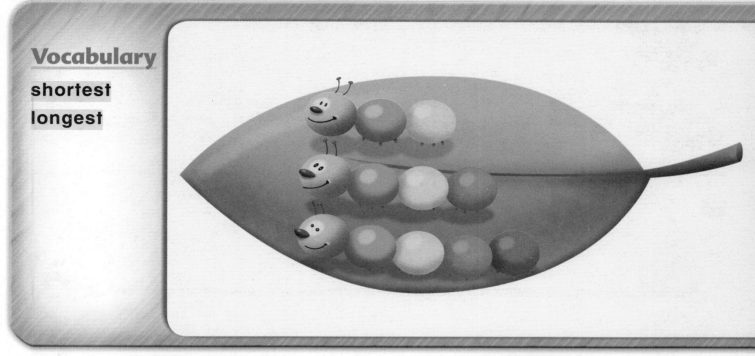

1.

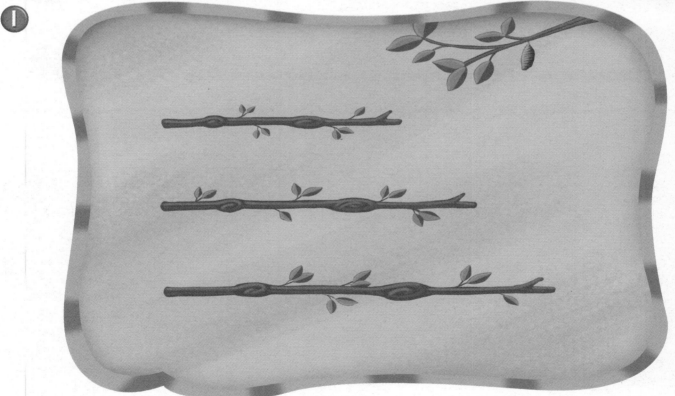

Directions:

1. Place 3 counters on the top twig. Trace the counters to make a caterpillar the same length as the twig.
   Place 4 counters on the middle twig. Trace the counters to make a caterpillar the same length as the twig.
   Place 5 or more counters on the bottom twig. Trace the counters to make a caterpillar the same length as the twig. Tell which caterpillar is shortest and which caterpillar is longest.

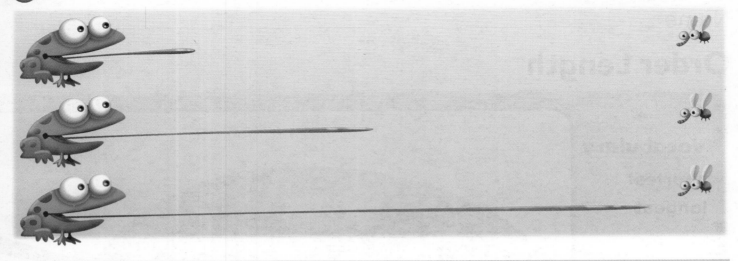

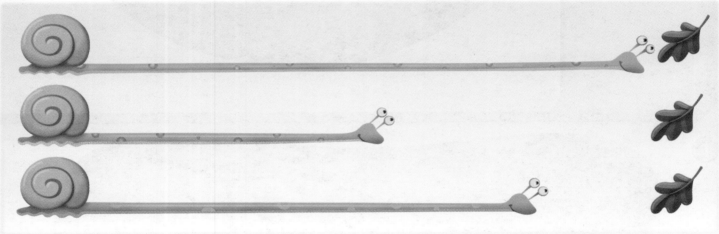

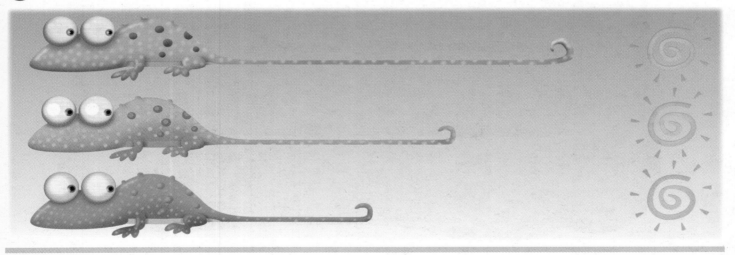

Directions:

2–4. Put a green X on the group of objects that is in order from shortest to longest. Put a blue X on the group of objects that is in order from longest to shortest. Put a red X on the group of objects that is not in order of length.

Math at Home Activity: Cut string into three strips of different lengths. Ask your child to order the strips from shortest to longest and from longest to shortest.

Name _____

Compare Weight

1

2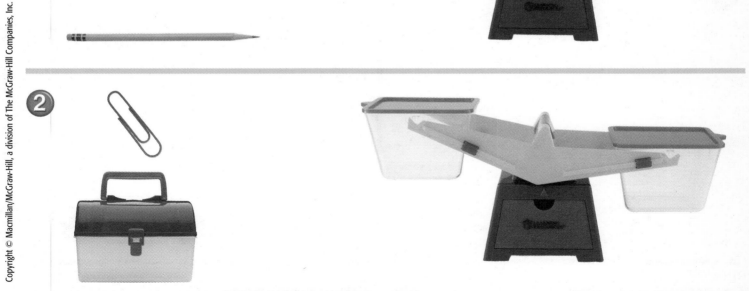

Directions:

1–2. Draw a line from each object to its correct place on the balance scale.

③

④

⑤

⑥

⑦

⑧

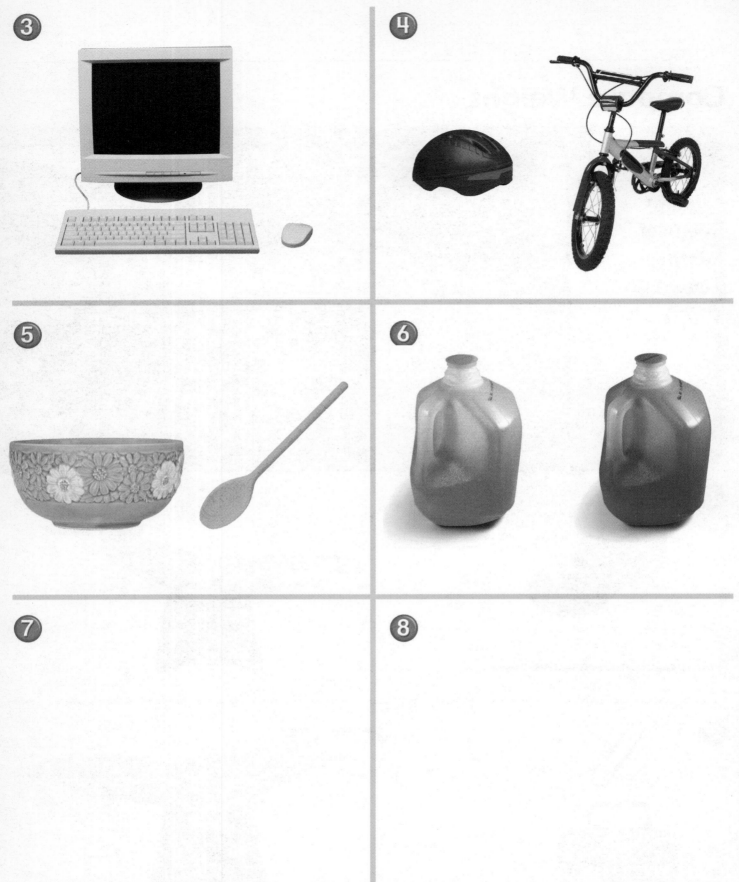

Directions:

3–6. Circle the heavier object.
Put an X on the lighter object. If the objects
weigh the same (or equal to), underline them.

7. Draw an object that is heavier than scissors.

8. Draw an object that is lighter than a chair.

Math at Home Activity: Use a canned good and empty cup.
Ask your child to close his or her eyes. Place one item in each of
your child's hands. Ask your child which hand holds the heavier
item and which hand holds the lighter item.

184 one hundred eighty-four

Chapter 7   Lesson 3

Problem-Solving Strategy
Guess and Check

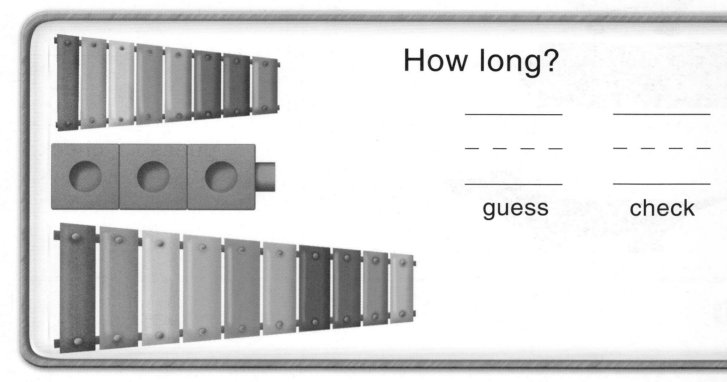

How long?

_____   _____

_ _ _ _ _ _ _ _   _ _ _ _ _ _ _ _

_____   _____

guess   check

1

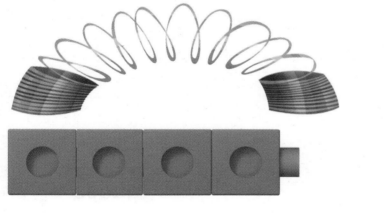

_____   _____

_ _ _ _ _ _ _ _   _ _ _ _ _ _ _ _

_____   _____

guess   check

Directions:

1. Circle the object that is longer. Then guess how many cubes long the longer object is. Is your answer close? Use cubes to check.

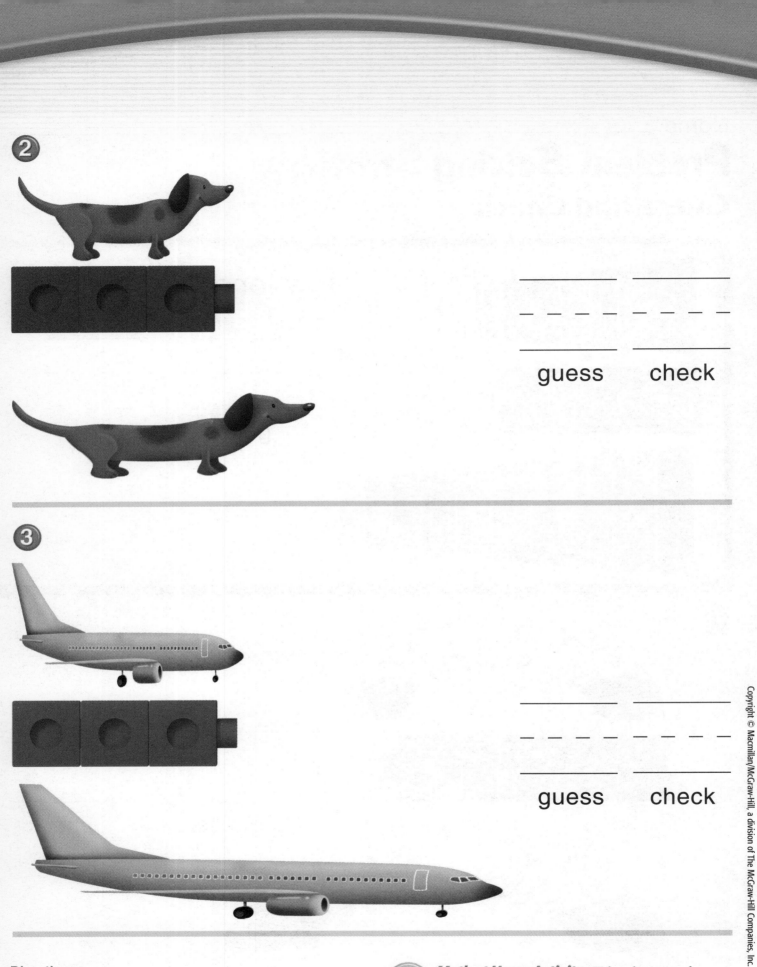

②

guess   check

③

guess   check

Copyright © Macmillan/McGraw-Hill, a division of The McGraw-Hill Companies, Inc.

Directions:

2–3. Circle the object that is longer. Then guess how many cubes long the longer object is. Is your answer close? Use cubes to check your guess.

 Math at Home Activity: Take advantage of problem-solving opportunities during daily routines such as riding in the car, bedtime, doing laundry, putting away groceries, planning schedules, and so on.

Chapter 7   Lesson 4

Name _____

1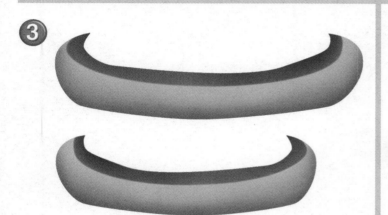

2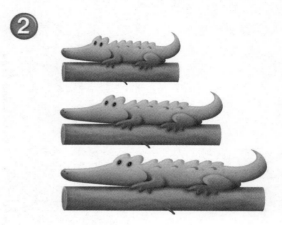

3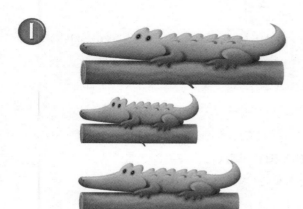

4

5

6

Directions:
1–2. Put a green X on the group of objects that are lined up from shortest to longest.
Put a red X on the group of objects that are not lined up from shortest to longest.
3. Circle the canoe that is longer. Put an X on the canoe that is shorter.
4–6. Circle the object that is heavier. Put an X on the object that is lighter. If the objects weigh the same underline them.

Chapter 7   one hundred eighty-seven   **187**

Building a Snake
Comparing Length

You Will Need

40

Play with a partner. Take turns
- Roll the cube.
- Move your counter that number of spaces.
- Collect the number of cubes shown on the space.
- Build a snake using the cubes.
- When you both reach Finish, compare the lengths of your snakes. The longer snake wins.

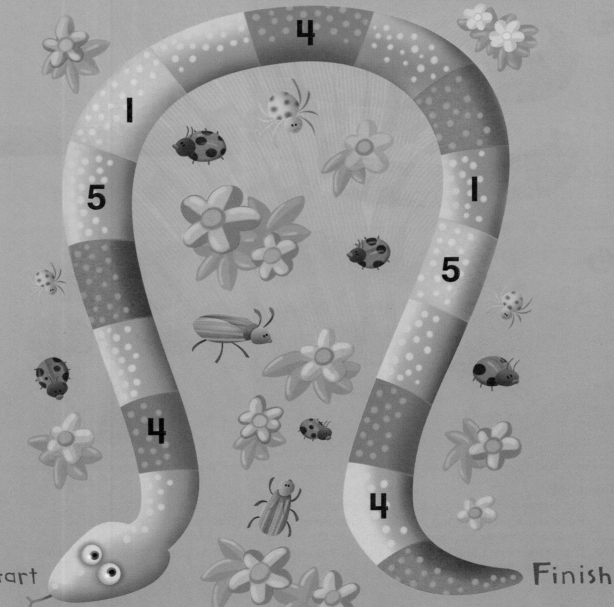

Start

Finish

Name _____

Compare Capacity

Copyright © Macmillan/McGraw-Hill, a division of The McGraw-Hill Companies, Inc.

Vocabulary

capacity
holds more
holds less
holds the
    same

1

2

Directions:
1–2. Circle the object that holds more.
Put an X on the object that holds less.

④

⑤

⑥

Directions:

3–6. Circle the object that holds more.
Put an X on the object that holds less.
If the objects hold the same, underline them.

Math at Home Activity: Use a small empty bowl and a large empty bowl. Have your child fill the small bowl with dry pasta. Pour the pasta from the small bowl into the large bowl. Ask your child which holds more.

Name _____

Compare Area

Vocabulary

area
covers more
covers less
covers the
 same

covers more ←   covers less →

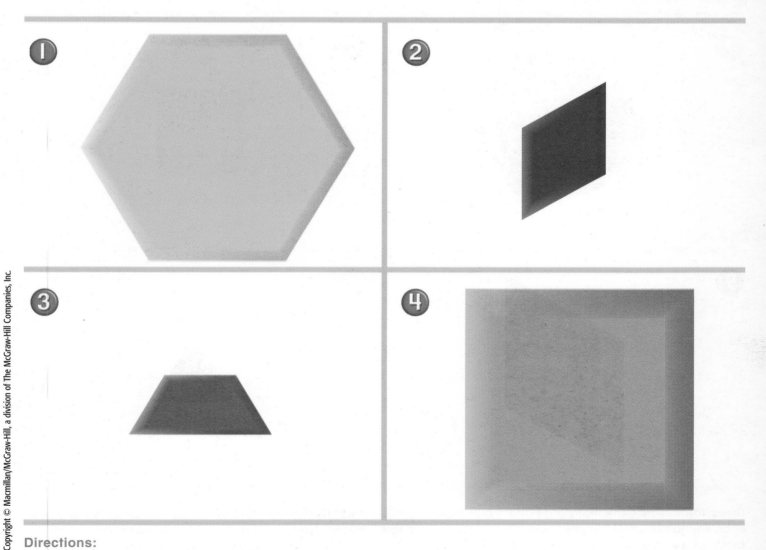

1

2

3

4

Directions:

Place the matching pattern block on each shape above. If the pattern block covers
more area than the shape, circle the shape. If the pattern block covers less area than the
shape, put an X on the shape. If the pattern block covers the same amount of area as
the shape, underline the shape.

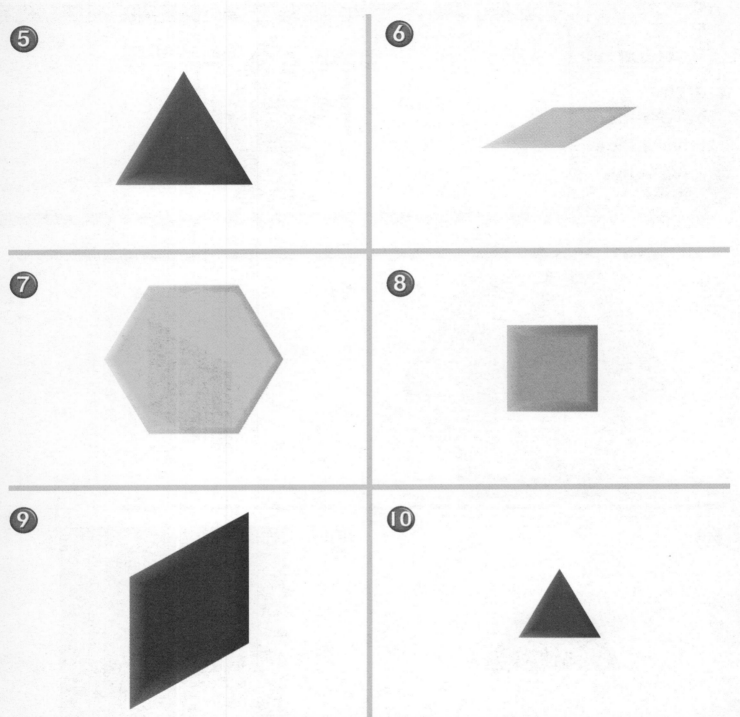

Directions: Place the matching pattern block on each shape above. If the pattern block covers more area than the shape, circle the shape. If the pattern block covers less area than the shape, put an X on the shape. If the pattern block covers the same amount of area as the shape, underline the shape.

 Math at Home Activity: Use an object, such as a book, and have your child determine if other objects around the house cover more, less, or the same area as the object.

Chapter 7   Lesson 6

Compare Temperature

Vocabulary

hotter
colder
temperature

 **Colder**

 **Hotter**

1

2

3

Directions:
1. Circle the object that is hotter.
2. Circle the object that is colder.
3. Name each object in the row. Circle the two
   objects that are about the same temperature.

Chapter 7   Lesson 7

④

⑤

⑥

Directions:
4. Circle the situation that is hotter.
5. Circle the situation that is colder.
6. Circle the two situations that are about the same temperature.

Math at Home Activity: Look in your cupboards or refrigerator. Name a food and have your child name a food you eat that is hotter than or colder than the one you chose. At dinner have your child name something he or she is eating that is hot and something he or she is eating that is cold.

What is your favorite flower?

_____

It may have grown
from a seed!

FOLD DOWN

D

Problem Solving
in Science

Real-World MATH

There are many types of flowers.

This book belongs to

_____

A

Some flowers grow from seeds.

Plant them. Watch them grow!

B

Which is the tallest? Circle your answer. Explain.

C

Name

①

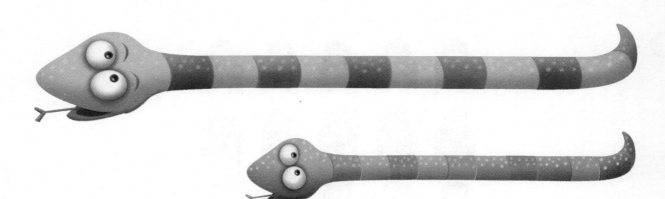

②

③

④

Directions:
1. Circle the object that is longer.
2. Put an X on the object that is heavier.
3. Put an X on the object that holds more.
4. Circle the object that is colder.

Name _____

 1

 2

3

Directions:
1. Count the objects. Write the number.
2. Identify the colored shape in the box. Circle the shapes in the group that are the same. Put an X on the shapes that are not the same.
3. Count the green buttons on the clown suits. Write the number.

Name _____

A.

○   ○   ○

B.

○   ○   ○

1.

○   ○   ○

2.   I5

○   ○   ○

Directions: Listen as the teacher reads the problem.
Choose the best answer.

Chapter 7   one hundred ninety-nine   **199**

3.

○　　　　　　○　　　　　　○

4.

7　　　　　　6　　　　　　4

○　　　　　　○　　　　　　○

5.

○　　　　　　○　　　　　　○

6.

○　　　　　　○　　　　　　○

STOP

Directions: Listen as the teacher reads the problem.
Choose the best answer.

Summative Assessment

Glossary/Glosario

English	A	Español

about

How many? about 20

aproximadamente

¿Cuántas hay? aproximadamente 20

above (page 71)

above

encima

sobra

add (page 283)

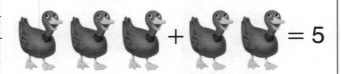

3 ducks   2 more join   5 ducks in all

sumar

3 patos   2 más se unen   5 patos en total

after (page 75)

6 is just after 5

después

5 6 7 8

El 6 sigue justo después del 5

Glossary/Glosario

English	A	Español

afternoon (page 227)

tarde

alike (same) (page 17)

alike different

semejante (igual)

semejante diferente

area (page 191)

covers more covers less

área

cubre más cubre menos

B

before (page 75)

5 6 7 8

6 is just before 7

antes

5 6 7 8

El 6 está justo antes del 7

A
B

Glossary/Glosario

English		Español

B

below (page 71)

below

abajo

abajo

beside

The dog is beside the cat.

al lado

El perro está al lado del gato.

between

between

entre

entre

big (bigger, biggest)

big   bigger   biggest

grande, más grande, el más grande

grande   más grande   el más grande

Glossary/Glosario

English	B	Español

bottom (page 73)

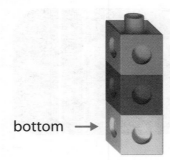

bottom →

fondo

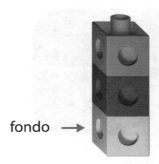

fondo →

C

calendar (page 233)

calendario

capacity (page 189)

holds more   holds less

capacidad

contiene más   contiene menos

Glossary/Glosario

English		Español

chart

Favorite Foods	
Food	Votes
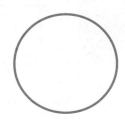	||||

tabla

Comidas Favoritas	
Comida	Votos
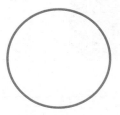	||||

circle (page 261)

círculo

cone (page 257)

cono

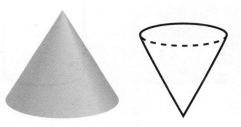

corner (page 263)

corner

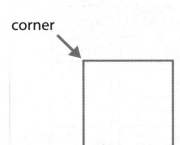

esquina

esquina

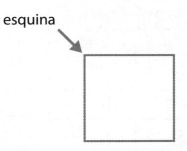

Glossary/Glosario

English		Español
	C	

count (page 43)

1	**2**	**3**
one	two	three

contar

1	**2**	**3**
uno	dos	tres

cube (page 257)

 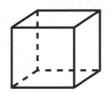

cubo

 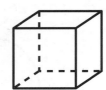

cylinder (page 257)

cilindro

D

data (page 131)

Favorite Foods	
Food	Votes
	||||
	|||
	|||| |||

information

datos

Comidas Favoritas	
Comida	Votos
	||||
	|||
	|||| |||

información

Glossary/Glosario

English		Español
	D	

different (page 17)

different   alike

diferente

diferente   semejantes

E

equal groups

3 in each group

grupos iguales

3 en cada grupo

equal parts (page 271)

partes iguales

equal sign (=) (page 341)

$$4 + 1 = 5$$

↑

equals

signo de igualidad (=)

$$4 + 1 = 5$$

↑

es igual a

Glossary/Glosario

English	E	Español

evening (page 227)

noche

G

graph (page 131)

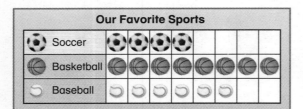

gráfica

Nuestros Deportes Favoritos							

group

A group of 4. →

A group of 3. →

grupo

Un grupo de 4. →

Un grupo de 3. →

Glossary/Glosario

English	**Español**

half (page 271)

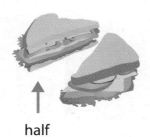

half

mitad

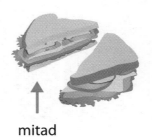

mitad

---

heavy (heavier, heaviest)

(page 183)

heavier

pesado (más pesado, el más pesado)

más pesado

---

height

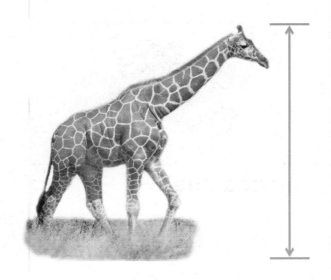

altura

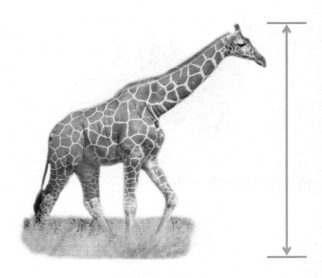

Glossary/Glosario

English		Español

H

holds less (page 189)

↑
holds less

contiene menos

↑
contiene menos

holds more (page 189)

↑
holds more

contiene más

↑
contiene más

L

length (page 179)

length

longitud

longitud

less than (page 31)

less than →

menos que

menos que →

Glossary/Glosario

English		Español
	L	

light (lighter, lightest)
(page 183)

lighter

liviano (más liviano, el más liviano)

más liviano

long (longer, longest)
(page 179)

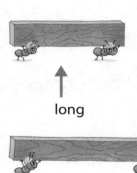

long

longer

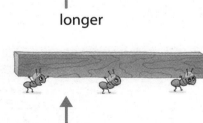

longest

largo (más largo, el más largo)

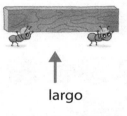

largo

más largo

el más largo

M

minus sign (–) (page 323)

$$5 - 2 = 3$$

minus

signo de sustracción (–)

$$5 - 2 = 3$$

menos

Glossary/Glosario

English		Español
month (page 233)	**M**	**mes**

month

mes

more than (page 29)

more than →

más que

más que →

morning (page 227)

mañana

Glossary/Glosario

English		**Español**

number (page 45)

número

1, 2, 3, 4, 5, 6, 7, 8, 9

1, 2, 3, 4, 5, 6, 7, 8, 9

numbers 1–9

números del 1 al 9

---

number line

recta numérica

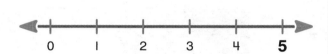

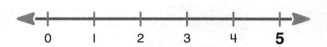

---

number sentence

expresión numérica

$2 + 1 = 3$

$2 + 1 = 3$

$3 - 1 = 2$

$3 - 1 = 2$

one-to-one correspondence

correspondencia directa

---

order (page 59)

orden

1, 3, 6, 7, 9

1, 3, 6, 7, 9

These numbers are in order
from smallest to largest.

Estos números están en orden
del menor al mayor.

Glossary/Glosario

English	Español

O

ordinal number (page 119)

first　second　third

número ordinal

primero　segundo　tercero

over (page 71)

over

sobre

sobre

P

pattern (page 77)

A, B, A, B, A, B

patrón

A, B, A, B, A, B

picture graph (page 139)

Our Favorite Toys

pictografía

Nuestros juguetes favoritos

Glossary/Glosario

English		Español
	P	

plus sign (+) (page 291)

$$5 + 2 = 7$$

↑

plus

signo de adición (+)

$$5 + 2 = 7$$

↑

más

	R	

real graph (page 133)

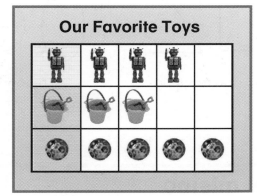

Our Favorite Toys

Real graphs have real objects on them.

gráfica real

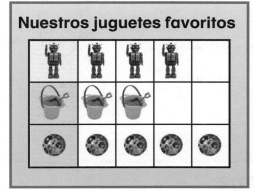

Nuestros juguetes favoritos

Las gráficas reales contienen objetos reales.

rectangle (page 261)

rectángulo

rectangular prism

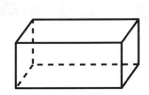

prisma rectangular

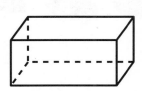

Glossary/Glosario

roll (page 259)

rodar

round (page 265)

not round   round

redondo

no redondo   redondo

S

same

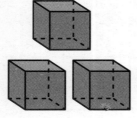

same color, same number

el mismo

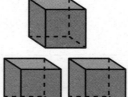 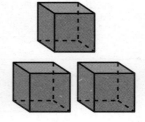

el mismo color, el mismo número

shape

figura

Glossary/Glosario

English	S	Español

short (shorter, shortest)
(page 179)

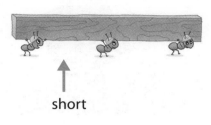

short

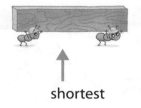

shorter

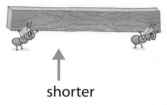

shortest

corto (más corto, el más corto)

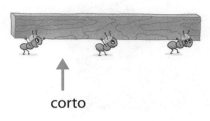

corto

más corto

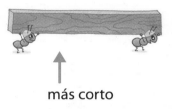

el más corto

side (page 263)

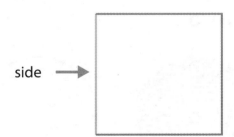

side →

lado

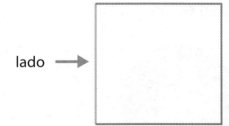

lado →

size (page 23)

small   medium   large

tamaño

pequeño   mediano   grande

Glossary/Glosario

English		Español

S

slide (page 259)

deslizar

sort (page 19)

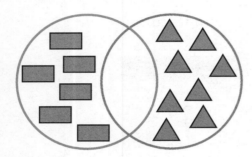

sorted or grouped by shape

ordenar

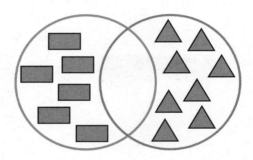

ordenado o agrupado por su forma

sphere (page 257)

 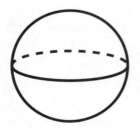

esfera

 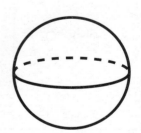

square (page 261)

cuadrado

Glossary/Glosario

English		Español

stack (page 259)

pila

---

subtract (subtraction)
(page 317)

5 take away 3 is 2. 2 are left.

restar (resta)

La resta de 5 menos 3 es 2. Quedan 2.

---

survey (page 141)

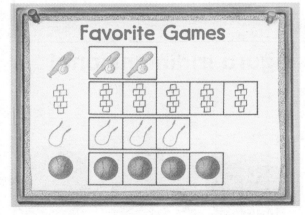

This graph shows the results from a survey.

encuesta

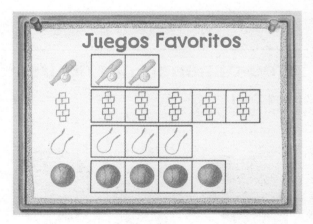

Esta gráfica muestra los resultados
de una encuesta.

Glossary/Glosario

English	Español
tall (taller, tallest)	**alto (más alto, el más alto)**

taller

más alto

temperature (page 193)	**temperatura**

hot   cold

caliente   frio

three-dimensional figure (page 257)	**figura tridimensional**

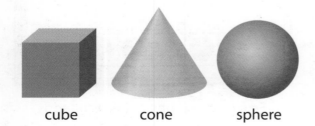

cube   cone   sphere

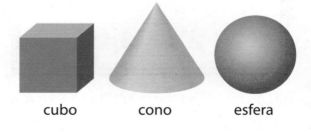

cubo   cono   esfera

Glossary/Glosario

today (page 231)

yesterday   today

hoy

ayer   hoy

tomorrow (page 231)

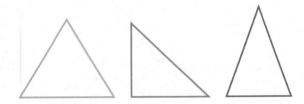

today   tomorrow

mañana

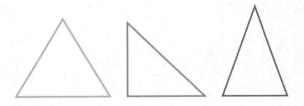

hoy   mañana

triangle (page 261)

triángulo

Glossary/Glosario

triangular prism

prisma triangular

two-dimensional figure

(page 261)

figura bidimensional

under (page 71)

debajo

under

debajo

Glossary/Glosario

W

week (page 229)

week

Sunday	Monday	Tuesday	Wednesday	Thursday	Friday	Saturday
		1	2	3	4	5
6	7	8	9	10	11	12
13	14	15	16	17	18	19
20	21	22	23	24	25	26
27	28	29	30			

April

semana

semana

domingo	lunes	martes	miércoles	jueves	viernes	sábado
		1	2	3	4	5
6	7	8	9	10	11	12
13	14	15	16	17	18	19
20	21	22	23	24	25	26
27	28	29	30			

abril

weight (page 183)

heavy   light

peso

pesado   liviano

Glossary/Glosario

Y

year (page 233)

January						
S	M	T	W	T	F	S
						1
2	3	4	5	6	7	8
9	10	11	12	13	14	15
16	17	18	19	20	21	22
23	24	25	26	27	28	29
30	31					

February						
S	M	T	W	T	F	S
		1	2	3	4	5
6	7	8	9	10	11	12
13	14	15	16	17	18	19
20	21	22	23	24	25	26
27	28					

March						
S	M	T	W	T	F	S
		1	2	3	4	5
6	7	8	9	10	11	12
13	14	15	16	17	18	19
20	21	22	23	24	25	26
27	28	29	30	31		

April						
S	M	T	W	T	F	S
					1	2
3	4	5	6	7	8	9
10	11	12	13	14	15	16
17	18	19	20	21	22	23
24	25	26	27	28	29	30

May						
S	M	T	W	T	F	S
1	2	3	4	5	6	7
8	9	10	11	12	13	14
15	16	17	18	19	20	21
22	23	24	25	26	27	28
29	30	31				

June						
S	M	T	W	T	F	S
			1	2	3	4
5	6	7	8	9	10	11
12	13	14	15	16	17	18
19	20	21	22	23	24	25
26	27	28	29	30		

July						
S	M	T	W	T	F	S
					1	2
3	4	5	6	7	8	9
10	11	12	13	14	15	16
17	18	19	20	21	22	23
24	25	26	27	28	29	30
31						

August						
S	M	T	W	T	F	S
	1	2	3	4	5	6
7	8	9	10	11	12	13
14	15	16	17	18	19	20
21	22	23	24	25	26	27
28	29	30	31			

September						
S	M	T	W	T	F	S
				1	2	3
4	5	6	7	8	9	10
11	12	13	14	15	16	17
18	19	20	21	22	23	24
25	26	27	28	29	30	

October						
S	M	T	W	T	F	S
						1
2	3	4	5	6	7	8
9	10	11	12	13	14	15
16	17	18	19	20	21	22
23	24	25	26	27	28	29
30	31					

November						
S	M	T	W	T	F	S
		1	2	3	4	5
6	7	8	9	10	11	12
13	14	15	16	17	18	19
20	21	22	23	24	25	26
27	28	29	30			

December						
S	M	T	W	T	F	S
				1	2	3
4	5	6	7	8	9	10
11	12	13	14	15	16	17
18	19	20	21	22	23	24
25	26	27	28	29	30	31

año

enero						
d	l	m	m	j	v	s
						1
2	3	4	5	6	7	8
9	10	11	12	13	14	15
16	17	18	19	20	21	22
23	24	25	26	27	28	29
30	31					

febrero						
d	l	m	m	j	v	s
		1	2	3	4	5
6	7	8	9	10	11	12
13	14	15	16	17	18	19
20	21	22	23	24	25	26
27	28					

marzo						
d	l	m	m	j	v	s
		1	2	3	4	5
6	7	8	9	10	11	12
13	14	15	16	17	18	19
20	21	22	23	24	25	26
27	28	29	30	31		

abril						
d	l	m	m	j	v	s
					1	2
3	4	5	6	7	8	9
10	11	12	13	14	15	16
17	18	19	20	21	22	23
24	25	26	27	28	29	30

mayo						
d	l	m	m	j	v	s
1	2	3	4	5	6	7
8	9	10	11	12	13	14
15	16	17	18	19	20	21
22	23	24	25	26	27	28
29	30	31				

junio						
d	l	m	m	j	v	s
			1	2	3	4
5	6	7	8	9	10	11
12	13	14	15	16	17	18
19	20	21	22	23	24	25
26	27	28	29	30		

julio						
d	l	m	m	j	v	s
					1	2
3	4	5	6	7	8	9
10	11	12	13	14	15	16
17	18	19	20	21	22	23
24	25	26	27	28	29	30
31						

agosto						
d	l	m	m	j	v	s
	1	2	3	4	5	6
7	8	9	10	11	12	13
14	15	16	17	18	19	20
21	22	23	24	25	26	27
28	29	30	31			

septiembre						
d	l	m	m	j	v	s
				1	2	3
4	5	6	7	8	9	10
11	12	13	14	15	16	17
18	19	20	21	22	23	24
25	26	27	28	29	30	

octubre						
d	l	m	m	j	v	s
						1
2	3	4	5	6	7	8
9	10	11	12	13	14	15
16	17	18	19	20	21	22
23	24	25	26	27	28	29
30	31					

noviembre						
d	l	m	m	j	v	s
		1	2	3	4	5
6	7	8	9	10	11	12
13	14	15	16	17	18	19
20	21	22	23	24	25	26
27	28	29	30			

diciembre						
d	l	m	m	j	v	s
				1	2	3
4	5	6	7	8	9	10
11	12	13	14	15	16	17
18	19	20	21	22	23	24
25	26	27	28	29	30	31

yesterday (page 231)

ayer

yesterday   today

ayer   hoy

April						
Sunday	Monday	Tuesday	Wednesday	Thursday	Friday	Saturday
		1	2	3	4	5
6	7	8	9	10	11	12
13	14	15	16	17	18	19
20	21	22	23	24	25	26
27	28	29	30			

abril						
domingo	lunes	martes	miércoles	jueves	viernes	sábado
		1	2	3	4	5
6	7	8	9	10	11	12
13	14	15	16	17	18	19
20	21	22	23	24	25	26
27	28	29	30			

Photo Credits

United States coin images from the United States Mint; **I** Grady Harrison/Alamy Images; **2** Jim Pickerell/Alamy Images; **3** Goran Kapor/Alamy Images; **4** (t)JoSon/Getty Images, (c)Richard Cummins/SuperStock; **5** Purestock/Getty Images; **7** Andy Jackson/Alamy Images; **9** (tl)Foodcollection/Getty Images, (others)The McGraw-Hill Companies; **I I** Paul J. Fusco/Photo Researchers; **13** Randy Lincks/Masterfile; **15** (tl)Brand X Pictures/PunchStock, (others)Eclipse Studios; **17** (party hat red cap stuffed rabbit)IndexOpen, (football helmet)Ryan McVay, (toy bear starfish pineapple goldfish)Getty Images, (orange)Stockdisc/PunchStock; **18** (t)CORBIS, (tcl)Getty Images, (others)Photos.com/Jupiterimages; **25** (t cr)Getty Images, (tc)Ryan McVay/Getty Images, (cl)CORBIS; **27** (t)Getty Images, (tc)IndexOpen, (c bcr)Masterfile, (bcl br)C Squared Studios/Getty Images, (bl)Chris Stock/Lebrecht/The Image Works; **32** (top to bottom)Stockdisc, CORBIS, Fielding Piepereit, Dave King/Getty Images, Photos.com/Jupiterimages, Masterfile; **33** (tcl)Getty Images, (tr)Photos To Go, (cr)The McGraw-Hill Companies, (b)The Stock Asylum, LCC/Alamy Images; **34** (t)Getty Images, (b)Richard Hutchings; **35** Getty Images; **36** Estelle Klawitter/zefa/CORBIS; **39** F. Lukasseck/Masterfile; **41** (tl)The McGraw-Hill Companies/Ken Karp, (others)Eclipse Studios; **42** (tl)The McGraw-Hill Companies/Ken Karp, (b)Richard Hutchings; **50** (tl)Kari Erik Marttila Photography, (tcl)BL Productions/SuperStock, (cl bl)Photos.com/Jupiterimages, (bcl)super stock; **57** (tcl)Ted Morrison/SuperStock, (tl)Photos.com/Jupiterimages, (cl)IndexOpen, (cr)Masterfile, (tr)SuperStock, (tcr)Tony Hutchings/Getty Images, (bcl)Leonard Lessin/Peter Arnold, Inc., (bl)photolibrary.com.pty.ltd/Index Stock, (br)James Urbach/SuperStock, (bcr)Peter Ardito/Index Stock; **58** (top to bottom)Masterfile, PunchStock, Alison Barnes Martin/Masterfile, IndexOpen, Getty Images, G.K. Vikki Hart/Getty Images, Ron Steiner/Alamy Images **61** (b)Tony Perrottet/Alamy Images, (t)CORBIS **62** (t)Jochen Sand/Getty Images, (b)Steve Niedorf Photography/Getty Images **64** (t)The McGraw-Hill Companies, (tcr c)G.K. & Vikki Hart/Getty Images, (c)The McGraw-Hill Companies/Ken Cavanagh, (b)Getty Images; **67** S Purdy Matthews/Getty Images; **69-70** Eclipse Studios; **85** (tl tr)Richard Hutchings (drum bell guitar)C Squared Studios/Getty Images, (maracas)George Doyle/Getty Images, (tambourine triangle)Getty Images;

86 (bl br)Richard Hutchings, (clarinet flute)C Squared Studios/Getty Images, (flute)Getty Images, (cymbal)Lebrecht Music and Arts Photo Library/Alamy Images; **89** (top to bottom)Ingram Publishing/Alamy Images, Digital Vision/Getty Images, Punchstock, Getty Images, Andrea Rugg/Beateworks/CORBIS; **90** (kite bike)C Squared Studios/Getty Images, (baseball)Getty Images, (paints)2006 JUPITERIMAGES, and its licensors. All rights reserved, (soccer ball)Ryan McVay/Getty Images; **93** Stockdisc/PunchStock; **95** Getty Images; **97** Image Source/SuperStock; **99-100** Eclipse Studios; **105** (t)C Squared Studios/Getty Images, (others)Mazer; **115** (fish)Alamy Images, (birds guinea pigs)G.K. & Vikki Hart/Getty Images, (yarn ball)Ken Cavanagh/The McGraw-Hill Companies, (cat post)Photospin/Imagestate, (bird seed bell)Mazer Corporation, (fish food)The McGraw-Hill Companies/Jacques Cornell; **116** (top to bottom)Comstock Images/Alamy Images, Mazer Corporation, Photospin/Alamy Images, Sergio Piumatti/Destinations, Getty Images, Kathleen Finlay/Masterfile, Getty Images; **123** (top to bottom)Getty Images, C Squared Studios/Getty Images, Brand X Pictures/Getty Images, C Squared Studios/Getty Images; **127** The McGraw-Hill Companies; **129** (cl)The McGraw-Hill Companies, (others)Eclipse Studios; **130** Eclipse Studios; **143** (t)Artifacts Images, (b)Ariel Skelley/CORBIS; **144** (cl)Paul Barton/CORBIS, (c)Richard Hutchings, Bruce Hershe /Jupiterimages; **146** (dragonfly)Creatas/PunchStock, (ladybug)D. Hurst/Alamy Images, (bell)C Squared Studios/Getty Images, (tambourine)Getty Images; **149** Raul Touzon/Getty Images; **151-152** Eclipse Studios; **155** Photos.com/Jupiterimages; **156** (tl)Photos.com/Jupiterimages, (t)Masterfile, (c)Stockdisc/PunchStock; **157** Photos.com/Jupiterimages; **158** Getty Images; **161** (l)Brand X Pictures/PunchStock, (cl r)Siede Preis/Getty Images, (cr)The McGraw-Hill Companies; **162** (l)D. Hurst/Alamy Images, (cl r)C Squared Studios/Getty Images, (c)Stockdisc/PunchStock, (cr)Don Farrall/Getty Images; **163-164** Stockdisc/PunchStock; **165** StudiOhio; **166** (cl)Getty Images, (others)StudiOhio; **169** (l)Brand X Pictures/PunchStock, (tl)Borland/PhotoLink/Getty Images, (tcl)Robert Glusic/Getty Images, (tcr)PhotoLink/Getty Images, (tr)MedioImages/Age Fotostock, (cl)CORBIS, (cr)BananaStock/PunchStock, (r)Creatas/Punchstock, (b)Richard Hutchings; **170** Beaconstox/Alamy Images; **172** (drum trumpet)Getty Images, (umbrella)Dave

Photo Credits

WorkMat 2

WorkMat 2: Two-Part Mat

WorkMat 3

WorkMat 4

WorkMat 4: Sorting Mat/T-Chart

WorkMat 5

WorkMat 5: Ten-Frame

WorkMat 6

WorkMat 6: Ten-Frames

Part

Part

Whole

WorkMat 7: Part-Part-Whole

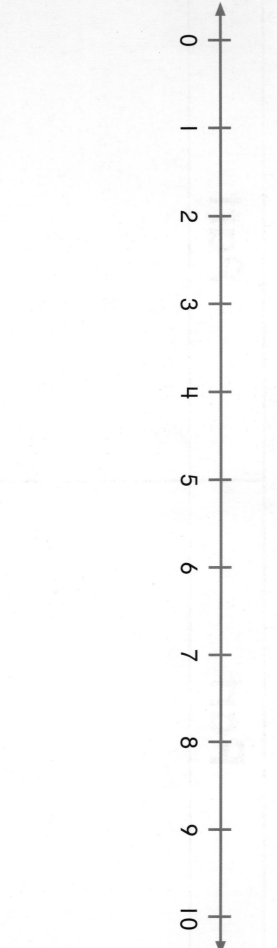

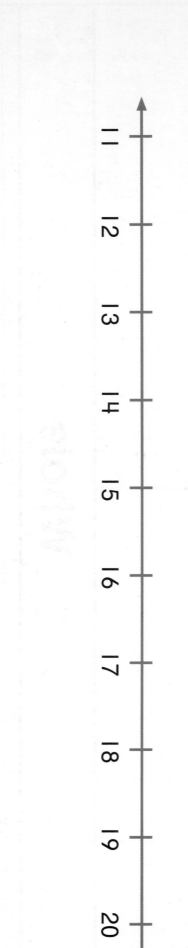

0 1 2 3 4 5 6 7 8 9 10

11 12 13 14 15 16 17 18 19 20

21 22 23 24 25 26 27 28 29 30

WorkMat 8: Number Lines